The Divine Hospital

SACRED MEDICINE

FOR THE

MODERN MIND

AN AYAHUASCA INITIATION IN BRAZIL

Eric Johnson

Foreword by Norberto Jurasek

☿ ☿ ☿

"But the net's unbreakable

So don't worry about falling

The voice that you ignore

Might be your future calling

Alone we're tossed about

Like a bottle in the sea

But together we ascend

And only then escape this gravity"

-Mercury, by Phish

Dedicated to the last remaining wilderness on Earth. May these places and the plants, animals and fungi living there receive the gratitude, protection and respect that they deserve. May the places already developed be restored to their original vibrant condition.

☿

Contents

After Brazil

Further

Foreword

Eric Johnson invites you to ask yourself, is there "something more than this?" It is perhaps the most significant question many of us can ask ourselves in the times we are at. In this question you might also read:

-Are you satisfied with the life you are living?
-Are you ready to take responsibility and create a life you want to live?

Human development is like a ladder of priorities. On one end there is safety, material well being, meaningful relationships, psychological health, inner peace, gratitude, a longing to share and contribute, meditation and enlightenment. On the other we find existential fear, misery, codependency, mental instability, inner turmoil, revengefulness and a wish to harm and destroy. Every step is valid.

This book is not for people in war zones, nor for the starving and certainly not for people struggling with severe mental disorders. They have other priorities.

This book is an inspiration. It is a sincere, experiential testimonial of someone like you, who is blessed to be already beyond the first step(s) of the ladder. Someone who has the intelligence to see the lack of satisfaction in the mental trance most people are in. Someone who is longing for "something more," for the real substance of life, and has had the courage to take action towards discovering it.

Technology, Big Bang, Moon, Mars, black holes, multiverses, neurology, biochemistry and so much more... It is all amazing and great! But it seems that we have been misled somewhere along the path too. I'm all for science, material well being, comfort and prosperity for everyone. But those alone have proven to be not enough for our beings to fly and enjoy the miracle that this life is. We are often like a bird trying to fly with just one wing, knowing deep down we are not fulfilling our natural development as human beings. And what is our natural development? Well, simply said, children should be joyous, adults learn with life, and in time become wise elders that lived fully and are ready to die in peace.

In native, uncontaminated traditions, elders are respected for their wisdom (not necessarily knowledge). They are a true source of guidance and active in decision making for the community. They live in high spirits. They are in love with life. They are connected with the earth. The good news is that quality of living is available to everyone who is ready, by stepping out of the ego to see and experience the simple goodness of life.

Foreword

This earth gives us all we need. It gives us the air and water. It gives us fruits and honey. It even gives us beautiful plants that help us to wake up and heal our wounds. There are many ways to come back to our hearts and to our natural self. Medicine work is one of them. It should be clearly stated that no one can say that it will be good for you. Either one hears the call or one doesn't, be careful.

This book can give you the opportunity to feel into it.

Enjoy!

-Norberto Jurasek, October, 2018
Facilitator/shaman and owner of Terramaya in Brazil.

Expectations

Terence McKenna once said, "Avoid gurus, follow plants,"which is quite ironic considering the man nearly achieved guru status to many of his admirers. If he were still alive today I'm sure he would remind the psychedelic community of the importance of these words. Terence often spoke of the need of the individual to find their own way down the spiritual path, with some guidance from the plants of course. There should be no middleman, priest, politician or CEO showing us the way because the truth can be experienced directly. Even the best of humans are imperfect; guilty of hidden bias, social conditioning or simple error that can lead us astray. There should be no middleman, however there can be a middle plant because the plants are free of ego, at least as far as I know, which makes them the perfect guru. Or perhaps we can all become gurus when the plants grant us access to a more silent mind that allows our Higher Selves to emerge. To make a long story short, I am not anybody else's guru, except perhaps my own. Sacred Medicines like Ayahuasca are far too complex for any human to fully understand. I doubt even a lifelong Shipibo shaman would ever claim to master Ayahuasca. Consciousness, life and Ayahuasca are all part of the great mystery that we fortunately have the opportunity to explore and experiment with. Nevertheless, I think a beginner will benefit from the information I am sharing, and someone more advanced can compare notes. You always have the option of testing somebody else's guidance to see if it is true for you. So with this book I offer you my opinions, insights and observations, which are based on years of working with Sacred Medicines, traveling to international psychedelic hot spots, attending conferences, following scientific research and connecting with members of the community. Having said that, any book is like a snapshot in time. It's important to remember that opinions change, new insights will emerge and more observations will be made. This is why I have included many gems of knowledge from my veteran shaman, a second opinion to confirm some of the ideas presented here.

This is a book about spiritual transformation. There are plenty of books available that attempt to explain exactly how Ayahuasca can provide healing in ways that conventional medicine often fails. I don't have the intention to repeat this type of work, so if the reader wishes to dive deeper into the science then there are options to choose from. This book focuses more on the experiential aspect of Ayahuasca than the molecular level. In this day and age we put so much faith in the MD's and PhD's of our society that we sometimes forget the value of good old-fashioned immersive learning. I'm sure there are many published authors who are far more familiar working in a clinical lab than they are lying on a mattress in a ceremonial space. The results gained from scientific analysis are certainly worth pursuing, but never underestimate the knowledge you gain from daily living, even if you don't have letters after your name or a certificate hanging on the wall.

At risk of stating the obvious, this would be a good place to make the disclaimer that many psychedelics are considered illegal substances by most governments of the world. The Sacred Medicines mentioned in this book were consumed in countries where they are protected by law. These days it is not uncommon to find underground Ayahuasca ceremonies in cities all around the world. Anybody seeking to participate should be aware of the local laws when you decide whether to partake. Even if you do have access to legal Sacred Medicines I would like to mention that this is serious business and may not be appropriate for all people. It is essential to consider your current state of mental, emotional and physical health before participating in a ceremony, though you don't need to be in perfect condition since people often come to the medicine for purposes of healing. Other factors to consider include the source or quality of the medicine; the setting or environment where the medicine will be consumed; and the facilitator or shaman serving the medicine.

I feel obligated to highlight this last point because it is a central theme of the book. Although in Brazil we drank without the guidance of a shaman I wouldn't recommend this approach to most people. This is not a case of arrogance, or do as I say, not as I do. In fact I am often humbled by the power these substances have and the recognition of how little I actually know. We only did this after years of working with Sacred Medicines and were still reluctant to drink alone despite the approval and encouragement of our shaman, who was very well aware of how we responded to challenging situations after monitoring us for years. He made it clear that the opportunity we had to drink alone would not be available for others in the future, so please don't ask.

This disclaimer is not meant to scare you away, rather to emphasize that intelligent and mindful decisions are necessary should you decide to pursue Sacred Medicines. Having said this, I strongly believe these plants and substances can lead us towards spiritual growth, improved health and a better world if we treat them with the respect they deserve. Many blessings to you as you travel down the Medicine Path.

☿

Before Brazil

More

"In a world gone mad, a world gone mad
There must be something more than this"

-More, by Trey Anastasio

There must be something more than this, but what exactly is the *more* he is referring to? Perhaps there could be more satisfaction in our lives, but how do we attain it? In this society *more* often means accumulating material possessions, but is that the best strategy for achieving satisfaction? We could buy a bigger TV, a faster car, sweeter ice cream or another pair of shoes. All of these things cost money, so we better get a higher paying job first if we want to be satisfied. Are rich people truly satisfied? Money can certainly help improve our lives, though it doesn't seem to be the ultimate solution. Despite living in one of the wealthiest countries in the world, millions of Americans are taking anti-depressants every day. There are also countless examples of famous wealthy people committing suicide, or addicted to substances. What about that higher paying job you got to buy all those nice things that were meant to buy you satisfaction? Do you want to spend all of your precious time working at that repetitious job you don't really like? If not, then let's break this cycle, try a different approach, and find out exactly what *more* means.

In the movie *Doctor Strange* the Ancient One tells the Doctor, "Arrogance and fear still keep you from learning the simplest and most significant lesson of all… it's not about you." Likewise, this book is not all about me, thank God. While it appears at first glance to only be a personal account of my psychedelic journey in Brazil, it's also a book for anybody who considers walking this path. The primary reason I wrote this is actually to awaken the reader to the possibility that you too can do the same. I obviously can't provide step-by-step instructions because that would lead you to my purpose, not yours. Rather this book demonstrates that another way is possible. I imagine that most people who suffer are either afraid of change and lack the confidence to attempt a similar feat, or have already accepted that there is nothing "more than this." To those afraid of change I hope this book motivates you to take action. To the others, there's nothing wrong with accepting your life as it is, except when "something more than this" does in fact exist but you have been conditioned to believe that it doesn't. One of my intentions is to show the reader that an elevated and expanded consciousness is attainable, not only for sages who meditate in a cave for fifty years in the Himalayas, but also for ordinary people seeking greater meaning in their life. In later chapters I will elaborate on this topic. This is not just some theory that I read in a book, I *know* there is something more than this, through direct personal experience. Regardless, you don't need to believe me, try a cup of Ayahuasca to see for yourself.

From my perception many people seem to be unfulfilled, like they are missing something but don't know what they are looking for. "There must be something more than this." I believe this intuition creates most of the anxiety and depression that have become so common in our society. Anxiety that leaves most people feeling like, being anywhere other than here and now. Depression that prevents people from seeing the beauty of life. These are some of the feelings that drove me to pursue a different path. In his masterpiece book *The Hero with a Thousand Faces*, scholar Joseph Campbell describes *the call* of the archetypal Hero's Journey as a person's strong desire to leave the comforts of home (society), an idea rarely understood by those living around them. The person can either follow the call or choose to ignore it. If they follow the call then there are certain to be monsters (fears and challenges) along the way, which must be faced if the hero is to succeed (grow). Eventually the hero returns home and discovers that the most difficult task of all is sharing the gift (knowledge) they received from completing the journey with those who never left home. I heard the call loud and clear as you are about to read, and this book is the gift I now share with those who are still deciding whether or not to be the hero of their own journey.

Consciousness is an extremely complicated subject that has been studied by some of the brightest minds in the world, and we still don't seem to fully understand what it is. From the perspective of Tibetan Buddhist monks to American medical doctors to Peruvian shamans to Swiss psychologists, there are many similarities and differences in their explanations of how it works. In order to have a discussion throughout the following chapters, we need to agree on a couple terms here. My basic assumption is that consciousness is broken into two components, the rational mind and the Higher Self. Perhaps that is an overly simplistic explanation, but at least it gives us a language to work with. For the sake of convenience, and for lack of a better word I will sometimes describe the Higher Self as a *state* of consciousness, a word that fails to capture the deeper meaning of this ineffable concept. The rational mind is the part of our consciousness that defines who we are. Also known as the ego, it forms an identity and insists that I am a white, male, American, non-religious, only child, university educated, author, who likes backpacking, dislikes barking dogs and owns an iPhone. Despite all these descriptions, the rational mind doesn't represent me because my Higher Self rises *above* them all. In the case of modern society the situation has been reversed as our Higher Selves have been obscured *beneath* a rational mind that has grown to dominate our existence. This may not sound like much of a problem since our science-driven, materialistic-oriented minds have developed into powerful tools over the centuries. However, the same minds that have accomplished amazing feats like building International Space Stations, or putting powerful mobile computers into our pockets, have also left us believing that we are our professions, possessions and nationalities. Borrowing from the work of Eckhart Tolle, we worry and fear non-stop without realizing that a greater version of ourselves exists if only we could turn down the volume on our internal chatter and be made aware of the Power of Now. Eckhart is trying to tell us that there is "something more than this," and it is related to discovering and becoming our Higher Selves.

It starts with the *Inception* of an idea, like a seed planted deep in your subconscious after seeing a beautiful photo on Facebook, having an inspiring conversation with a friend or watching a great movie. As time passes that seed becomes an active thought that is watered by the encouragement of others through newly discovered podcasts, books and music. The weeds of fear and doubt are pulled away and the young idea is given space to break through the soil and grow. Eventually the sun shines upon the newly formed leaves and gives energy to develop a plan and make changes. How big that plant becomes and what fruits it produces are for you to decide. It's not about me. The focus has shifted from my personal journey towards helping people on their own journey. It's time to spread the seeds and see what new growth emerges. Sometimes birth comes from death like tomatoes growing on composted kitchen waste or mushrooms spreading through a fallen tree. In my case the death of my old lifestyle needed to happen before I could become who I am today. A radical decision to quit my job and head for the Amazon rainforest of Peru three years ago in pursuit of healing through Ayahuasca was an important first step along my journey to find "something more than this."

☿

*** The following two chapters were written two years *after* my first trip to Peru, and one year *before* our trip to Brazil.

Leaving my Job

"And may the best of your todays be the worst of your tomorrows
And may the road less paved be the road that you follow"

-Have It All, by Jason Mraz

Some would say I had it all. I certainly was not wealthy by American standards, but by world standards I was quite successful. I had a stable and permanent job with the federal government, which is known for offering generous benefits including retirement, health insurance, paid leave, sick time and holidays. I lived in a small city with a high quality of life, easy access to nature, many organic food stores and a population of progressive people. It was large enough to offer some of the amenities that make life interesting, yet there was minimal noise, traffic and pollution. My apartment had a beautiful view of the bay, and was within walking distance to a vibrant downtown. I owned a reliable car for trips to places like the pristine national park that was only a couple hours away. I also had a loving girlfriend, and a close friend who had much in common. Yet I gave it all away for an extended trip to Peru. Was it a foolish decision? Perhaps, but first consider my reasons for leaving before you answer.

I had reached the limits of my patience with a job that was leading me nowhere. There was little possibility of advancing further in the agency, or learning more skills to become a better employee. The job was nothing more than a way of paying my bills, as many jobs are. The repetitive nature of the work, my uninspiring coworkers and the dark rainy climate of the region left me feeling depressed. Sitting in an office and staring at a computer screen all day was draining the life energy from my body. Sunday evenings my mood would steadily decline as I was reminded of the workweek ahead. The long commute to the office tormented me. My applications for open positions with other organizations were being ignored. I requested and was granted a shortened four-day workweek, which helped me to tolerate the situation, but didn't relieve the depression. I wondered, is this all there is to life??? I wanted to reach my full potential and that definitely was not happening in my position. Something had to change soon.

In addition to my existential crisis, I had been suffering from rare food sensitivities that resulted in huge swellings on my skin. I clearly remember the first time it happened, shortly after accepting a new job that I quickly discovered was not a great match. I had woken up to go to work one morning and sensed that something was wrong. I looked in the mirror and was shocked to see my upper lip resembling a large sausage. The skin stretched so tight that it appeared to nearly tear. After that day the reactions continued for years. The worst part was not knowing exactly which foods were to blame, or when the next swelling would occur. Conventional medicine's solution was to treat the reactions with pharmaceuticals, but I immediately dismissed this option. Having been trained in Ayurveda, a traditional system of medicine from India that emphasizes the importance of a proper diet, I knew that it is better to treat the source of disease rather than the symptoms. Fortunately an Ayurvedic practitioner showed me what types of food I was sensitive to, which was extremely helpful because I could now avoid the culprits. Unfortunately this removed over fifty percent of the common diet from my plate, including dairy, grains, legumes, seeds and nuts, which as you can imagine makes eating quite a challenge. My practitioner showed me the foods responsible for my reactions, but not the reason why my body was rejecting them. I wanted to find the solution.

As Steve Jobs once said during a Stanford commencement speech, "You can't connect the dots looking forward, you can only connect them looking backwards." I can now see the dots that connected me to a powerful Sacred Medicine known as Ayahuasca. I had been practicing Brazilian Jiu Jitsu and one of my training partners introduced me to Joe Rogan who is an avid martial artist among other roles. Through his podcast I was introduced to many fascinating guests including Aubrey Marcus, Dan Engle and Dennis McKenna. All of these men introduced me to Ayahuasca for the first time. Their discussions of the potential benefits of Ayahuasca grabbed my attention and I quickly realized that it wasn't enough for me to sit around listening to others speak of this mystical vine; I needed a direct experience. I was going to drink this exotic brew in the plant's native home, the Amazon rainforest.

I had enough vacation time saved up to take a three-week paid leave from work. In the United States not all employers offer paid vacation so there are many people that can't afford to be away from work for even two weeks per year. Compared to them I was certainly fortunate. Despite this generous opportunity I was seeking a more radical transformation in my life than a three-week break followed by a return to the old routine, so I decided to resign from my position. I like to call it a preemptive action against a mid-life crisis. Why wait for the crisis to happen? As I learned from Ayurveda, it's better to prevent disease than to react to it, so leaving in relatively good health sounded preferable to waiting ten more years until I broke down and burned out. This decision raised many difficult questions. If not three weeks then how long should the trip be? Do I buy a one-way plane ticket? Should I sell all my possessions, or put them in storage? How to deal with the strain on my relationship? And of course, how will I earn an income when I return from the Amazon?

It was time to swallow the Red Pill and unplug from *The Matrix*. I wanted to improve my health. I wanted to find meaningful and satisfying work. I wanted to experience Ayahuasca. I wanted to evolve spiritually. In order to accomplish these lofty goals I decided it was necessary to walk away from it all, and to do that there were a few important prerequisites. First, I was debt free, an increasingly rare concept in this credit driven society. By living a minimalist lifestyle and separating my needs from wants I was able to save enough money over the years for the trip, and the unemployment that followed. Second, I was child free, also rare for a man in his late thirties, and part of the reason I was debt free. However, my girlfriend was not child free, which prevented her from coming along and made my decision to follow my passion more difficult. Finally, being a home renter rather than an owner and having no pets or other major responsibilities certainly made my trip much easier.

Just as Joe Rogan led me to Ayahuasca in the Amazon, the dots continued to connect me to Huachuma (San Pedro cactus) in the Andes where I met a marvelous woman named Phoenyx during a full moon ceremony. She introduced me to an amazing network of people who I now call my Sangha, or community. My old relationship came to a painful end, and a new one began. I stayed in Peru the maximum time I was allowed, three months instead of the three-week vacation that I originally considered. The journey never really ended after leaving Peru and extended back to the US. Phoenyx joined me in other beautiful places like the energetic red rocks of Sedona, the giant redwood trees and Mount Shasta of California, the mossy green rainforests of the peninsula in Washington, and so on. Together our explorations of Sacred Medicines expanded beyond Ayahuasca and Huachuma to other substances like Peyote, Psilocybin Mushrooms, MDMA and LSD. Throughout all of this I lived by my rules and followed my schedule rather than those of my employer, which was extremely satisfying.

During my quest to discover and eliminate the source of my food reactions I initially focused on the physical body. My efforts included a combination of Kambo frog poison therapy, juice fasts, yoga, massage, high elevation hikes in the Andes, and of course strong doses of plant medicines like Ayahuasca. In addition, replacing the daily routine of sitting in front of a computer all day at the office with moving through an exotic landscape was very therapeutic. While all my attention was on physically detoxing my body I was pleased to notice the improvements in my mind and spirit emerging. The cold defensive wall surrounding my heart began to slowly melt and emotions were felt. Past traumas were processed and removed. Stored energies were released in the form of leg shaking and an epic *Incredible Hulk* yell. I even had the pleasure of experiencing a spiritual awakening for one unforgettable day.

There is no turning back from the radical lifestyle transformation that I chose, yet two years after the trip a question that naturally arises is, was it worth leaving my job for Ayahuasca? I still haven't replaced the last job with a better one, and the stress and uncertainty of not knowing where I'm heading next has been quite a challenge. Although it definitely came at a cost, I have no regrets about my decision to walk away from it all. Having a savings account has helped me avoid taking an undesirable job out of desperation. The food sensitivities remain, however this physical condition should be seen as the fuel that drove me to Peru and led to my emotional and spiritual development. I exchanged comfort and stability for adventure and magic. I try to remember that healing and growth happens on a timeline beyond my control and I can't expect to solve a lifetime of issues in a single trip. The people, places and experiences that I have encountered while walking this Medicine Path have certainly added great depth to my life.

In the next chapter I will share with you how I dealt with the transition of returning home following a profound three-month transformational journey to Peru.

☿

Life After Ayahuasca

Praise Jesus, praise Buddha, rejoice, you've seen the light!!! You just finished a ten-day retreat in the rainforest and have a new perspective of life. For the first time you see beyond the veil of illusion that has been obscuring your vision for all these years. You purged toxins that have been in your system so long that you forgot what it's like to feel healthy. After living in a crowded concrete city for decades you gained a new appreciation for the color green and the abundance of life that is the rainforest. You experienced a sense of peace forgotten long ago and realize this is how life is supposed to be. And in a few days you are catching a flight to Lima before connecting to that long international flight back home… then, what happens next?

When you return home there is a strong temptation to tell anybody willing to listen about what you have just experienced. You seriously consider climbing atop the nearest roof and shouting for all to hear. Standing in the middle of the city plaza and asking people to gather around seems like a real option. You want to share your revelations with all your friends in a Facebook post. At the very least you will certainly give your family a full update of your adventures while sitting around the dinner table, "Mom you really need to try this!"

Trust me, I totally understand that urge to spread the word far and wide. Ayahuasca and other powerful Sacred Medicines like Huachuma, Iboga, Psilocybin Mushrooms and Peyote are what the world needs most right now. You could even say our survival as a species depends on them. My strategy has mostly been to share only with the people that truly want to know and avoid isolating myself too much from the rest who may view my actions and beliefs as strange. I eventually came out of the Psychedelic Closet, and lean strongly towards, "This is who I am, love it or leave it," but still think it is wise to be tactful about the subject. Let's not forget that while Ayahuasca may now seem as normal and necessary to us as drinking water we still live in a society that considers it to be an exotic illegal *drug*.

One of the most confusing social situations for me since returning from South America is trying to answer the question that is inevitably asked, exactly what were you doing in Peru? I could say that I was hiking through the Andes while drinking Pisco Sours and taking selfie photos with llamas at Machu Picchu. Or I could tell the truth, which is I left my job to legally drink one of the most potent mind-altering substances known, which caused me to vomit and see the world as it really is. To recognize that: we live in a democracy owned by corporations that pay politicians to make decisions that bring greater profit rather than actually help the citizens who elected them; our economic system is dependent on never ending growth which is devouring our natural resources at a rate faster than they can regenerate and polluting the environment we depend on for survival; we are on a quest to buy our way to happiness through the consumption of material products that the corporations convince us we need through clever psychological advertisements; college debt, home mortgages and credit cards are forever enslaving us to soul sucking office jobs that create sicknesses we try and treat with ineffective pharmaceuticals that only suppress the symptoms and cause terrible side effects; humans are responsible for one of the largest extinction events in the history of this planet. Yeah, that's what I was doing in Peru, lovely weather we're having today, did you see the game last night, what's new with you?

I know how cynical that must sound, but the purpose is to highlight the extreme contrast between previewing our full potential as human beings during ceremony and then returning to a society that appears to be sick and insane. Remember that even though you may have radically changed, the home you return to will be relatively the same. Finding employment that is in alignment with my values has been a struggle for me since I came back. I always thought that swallowing the Red Pill and unplugging from *The Matrix* would be the difficult part, but now I see that coming back is the real challenge. I suppose that Neo never tried to come back to his office job, but we all have bills to pay, right? How can I be part of the solution rather than the problem? How can I be of service to others using my new perspective on life? And so the search continues to find meaningful work that supports a healthy and sane lifestyle and society.

We've all heard how important it is to integrate after ceremony. Psychedelics are very effective at dis-integrating our lives. They tear apart some of our beliefs and habits by disrupting outdated thought patterns. They also act as a mirror that confronts us with how we have been living and show us where improvements are needed. In the beginning I only thought of integration as those days following ceremony where it is crucial that we get plenty of rest, drink clean water, breathe fresh air, eat a healthy diet and take quiet walks in nature. Proper integration also means avoiding travel, stress, media and negative people as much as possible. This could be called the first phase of integration, the time when you are returning from the spiritual realm back to the physical and reforming as a person with recently gained insights.

I now see the second phase of integration that extends weeks and even months after ceremony as being equally important. The second phase includes returning home, finding a community you can relate to, creating a new lifestyle and deciding what service you will provide to others. Drinking is the easy part, putting the pieces back together is the real challenge, especially for those who take seriously the messages they receive from the vine. This is one of the major differences between plants and pharmaceuticals, the necessity to do more than simply swallow. For maximum benefits it's important to take action after ceremony and implement the lessons learned into your daily routine. Integration is a real challenge, but it is also an opportunity to create a better version than the original, which is after all the reason we first went to the rainforest.

☿

*** The remainder of the book was written during and shortly after Brazil.

Evicted

The uncertainty continued nearly two years following my return to the US from an epic three-month trip to Peru. The only certainty was that I wanted to walk down the Medicine Path wherever it was taking me. Prior to visiting Peru I heard the call of Sacred Medicines and knew that "There must be something more than this" life than I had previously discovered. After visiting Peru I realized that the medicines were the *more* that I had been seeking. For some people the medicines show the *more* in the form of improved relationships, connection to nature or simply feeling better. For others the medicines *are* the *more*, either in the form of researching them at a university, advocating for them through a non-profit, serving them to people as a facilitator or countless other possibilities. I knew that I wanted to work with the medicines, but still did not know exactly how. To make the situation more difficult was the fact that they were mostly illegal and unknown in my country. Ever since I graduated from high school I have been on a lifelong mission to find a career that not only paid the bills, but also one that supported my health, matched my interests and felt rewarding. As if that wasn't idealistic enough, I wanted to earn an income by contributing to a better world, instead of exploiting people or planet. This is no easy task, especially in this complicated and highly connected world where one action always leads to a consequence, expected or unexpected, regardless of our intentions. I soon realized that working with these medicines could fulfill all these requirements and allow me to complete my mission.

The uncertainty of what my role would be in the medicine field made the rest of my life confusing to say the least. I knew that I would attend as many ceremonies and conferences as possible, and consume as many books and films as I could find in order to gain experience and knowledge about my new passion. What about the more foundational aspects of life though, such as what city to live in and how to earn money? Having no family or home mortgage gave me infinite possibilities of where to go and what to do. I had still been applying to conventional jobs as a bridge to get closer to my passions. What if I signed a yearlong apartment lease in Bellingham and then got accepted for a job in Portland? For this reason I floated around for a year and a half and avoided any commitments that didn't look promising. There were a few odd jobs along the way including a short and painful attempt at delivering mail for the Postal Service in Washington. I volunteered as an Ayurvedic cook for a yoga teacher school in Sedona. I also tried working as a wilderness therapy instructor in Oregon. But it seemed that I reached a point where self-employment was the only viable option remaining. The good news is that I had the freedom to see much of the West Coast from the redwoods of California all the way up to the rainforests of Washington. I wouldn't recommend this approach to others unless you happen to be extremely adaptable to uncertainty. The lack of grounding was difficult and left me craving simple things like the peace and privacy of my own apartment. Eventually I returned to Washington once again and found a roommate situation that didn't require signing a lease.

For the first time in months I settled down and sunk some roots into the soil. It felt good, but I knew it was not a permanent solution and continued my search for what to do next. Finally after nine months change came my way in the form of an eviction notice. No, I'm not a bad guy; I didn't get kicked out for having loud late night parties or neglecting to pay the rent. Rather I chose not to sign a lease and therefore gave my roommate the option of replacing me with a close friend in need of shelter who she would prefer to live with. No hard feelings, a temporary place to live is what I wanted and a temporary place to live is what I got, but now what? I had about forty days to answer that question with no serious opportunities available.

Meanwhile Phoenyx had spent the prior year going through the process of an early retirement from the police department in Germany and spent her free time volunteering as an assistant at Ayahuasca workshops. After years of drinking the medicine as a participant with different facilitators in Europe and Peru, she had unofficially graduated to the next level. She was ready to give back following the healing she had received from Ayahuasca for

Post Traumatic Stress Disorder (PTSD), which I will speak about in later chapters. An assistant doesn't have the responsibility of a shaman, but does play an important role during the ceremony. They are the volunteers who support workshop participants who are struggling during exceptionally difficult experiences, help set up and clean up the ceremony space, empty vomit buckets and bring people to the toilet when they can't walk.

The shaman she was assisting was a Brazilian man named Norberto who would probably prefer the title of facilitator or Ayahuasquero because he does not operate as a traditional shaman would. A traditional shaman might work directly one on one with the participant by singing songs to them, beating a drum or moving their energy in some way. Some neo-shamans like Norberto take a more hands off approach and allow the participant to go through the ceremony independently. He pours the medicine and generally monitors the ceremony to make sure everybody is safe from beginning to end. When a participant is really struggling he is there to guide them through the process, but other than that the primary relationship is between the participant and the medicine. Ayahuasca is the real healer and he tries to stay out of the way as much as possible. I definitely prefer this style over all others I've experienced. Some neo-shamans put restrictions on the participants and try to control their behavior by requesting that they remain silent, avoid dancing, etc. While it is true that an out of control participant could be a distraction to others in the ceremony I believe that the greatest healing occurs when we don't feel judged or censored. Norberto's background includes many years spent with the Santo Daime church in

Brazil, and the teachings of the Indian mystic Osho. He has also studied Bioenergetic Analysis Therapy, Relationship Codependency, breathwork and meditation. The Santo Daime church originated in Brazil and is a hybrid that combines Catholicism with Ayahuasca. His mentor at the church was a woman named Baixinha who is largely responsible for steering him back on course when his life was heading in the wrong direction as a young man, and played a major role in teaching him the ways of Ayahuasca. Despite his church background I never detected the presence of Catholicism during his ceremonies, which was perfect for me since I don't consider myself religious. He had nearly all the ingredients I was looking for in a facilitator.

Anyway, back to the eviction. Soon after receiving notice to move out of the apartment Phoenyx sent me a message from the workshop she was assisting at. She said that Norberto invited us to be caretakers for his property in Brazil while he was away traveling. I couldn't believe it; I was scheduled to move December 1, but still had no plans, and was now invited to be caretaker beginning December 8! The timing was incredible and just as one door closed another one opened. Better yet, in addition to offering us free food and lodging he promised to leave a bottle of Ayahuasca that we could drink in the temple during his absence. This was a bit shocking for me, as I had always assumed that Ayahuasca should only be consumed under the expert guidance of a shaman. While we had gone through ceremonies alone before with many other medicines the thought of drinking Ayahuasca alone never crossed my mind. Regardless, it was an amazing opportunity to learn more about Sacred

Medicines in a country where they are legal, and the timing couldn't be any better. It reminded me of La Chorrera, the small village Terence McKenna and his brother Dennis visited in the Colombian rainforest as young men. The two pushed the limits of human consciousness during that trip, a feat that I had no desire to repeat, but the similarities between our journeys couldn't be ignored, and it didn't take long for me to name the trip "Our Chorrera."

The following few weeks were dedicated to preparing for my first trip to the Atlantic Rainforest of Brazil. Fortunately I had already purchased the required Brazilian Visa earlier that year in anticipation of a potential upcoming workshop on Norberto's property, otherwise it would come at a higher cost to acquire one on such short notice. I moved my few possessions into storage, packed my bags and said my goodbyes. In forty days my status changed from evicted to invited to confirmed, for my flight to Rio de Janeiro.

Well, that is my entire life from Peru leading up to Brazil summarized in a few short chapters. What follows takes place on Norberto's property, so to begin this section I'd like to share the opening prayer for his ceremonies. These words come to us as a message from Tupinamba, a native of Brazil:

Evicted

Life

Health

Happiness

Open paths

Health in the body

Peace in the spirit

And love in the heart

It is this that we wish

For ourselves

For our loved ones

And for all of our brothers and sisters

So be it

And with these words, the ceremony (and this section of the book) is open. You may now drink the Mother, Ayahuasca (or the words to follow).

☿

Brazil, Part One

Arrival

From the airport I followed the directions Norberto had sent me, and through a series of bus transfers I arrived a few hours later in the town where we had agreed to meet. Through the bus window I saw him waiting at the stop for my arrival. Brazil has a great diversity of races and is mostly represented by Africans, Indigenous and Portuguese who have mixed through the centuries. Because of this it's difficult to describe what a typical Brazilian looks like. Norberto is in his forties, has light skin, medium height, a thin frame and long wild black hair, at least what remains. Most memorable are those big brown gentle, yet penetrating eyes that those of us who have drunk with him before know so well. The kind of eyes that look to the back of your soul, and give you a complete scan before agreeing to pour you another shot of Ayahuasca for the night. He doesn't wear brightly colored feathers or tribal clothes that grab your attention, yet there is an extreme presence about him if you know what to look for. At first glance it might be difficult to believe this simple looking man can help guide people through some of the most challenging, strange and beautiful situations they will ever experience in their lives, yet he does so in a masterful way.

We hopped in his truck and during the ride I watched the paved road turn into a dirt road, which later turned into a bumpy dirt road. "Wow Norberto, this road is getting rough, your place must be isolated," I said. "Yes," he replied with a big grin on his face, as if he took great pride in living beyond the reach of civilization, and then added with his melodic Brazilian accent, "but we are not there yet." Soon the houses along the rough road began to appear less frequently and I repeated the comment, "Wow Norberto, your place must be *very* isolated," and again he seemed quite pleased with my realization. Eventually we reached a point where there were no more houses along the road, and I could only see the dark green Atlantic Rainforest surrounding us along with the occasional view of a river rushing below. The need for a four-wheel drive truck became apparent as we drove through a swampy section of road surrounded by fragrant white flowers. We parked at the end of the road and as I stepped outside the vehicle, I noticed how warm, moist and thick the air was, similar to entering a greenhouse. It smelled of vegetation and was pure in contrast to the air I had been breathing on the long flight across the ocean. Once again he told me, "We are not there yet," so I grabbed my heavy backpack, crossed a bridge and noticed what appeared to be a large *Brugmansia* shrub growing near the stream. It was covered in the white trumpet shaped flowers that immediately distinguish the plant from others. Although it wasn't my cup of tea, some shamans in the Amazon work with this extremely powerful plant, which they call Toé. Only a few minutes on the property and I was already seeing Sacred Medicines growing freely.

As we began walking up a steep trail towards the property, Norberto moved quickly with his small pack as he hurried to drop me off before sunset. He had other business to take care of back in town, and wanted to get me situated before it was dark. I moved slowly following a long transcontinental flight, but wanted to show that I was fit for duty as caretaker of this wild land, so I picked up the pace and pushed myself up that hill. There were tall banana plants in the surrounding forest along with thick vines climbing the trees, and multiple species of plants growing in the canopy high above the ground. I began to sweat as my heart rate increased. Eventually he stopped to give me a breather and showed me some Ayahuasca vines that were growing hidden among the many other plants. I could see that he was very happy to show me the plants growing there that would someday be cooked and used for ceremony when they were mature. Until then Norberto would need to import his medicine from other parts of Brazil. The thought of drinking medicine that had been grown and prepared from the same land where we would be staying was very appealing, comparable to eating fresh tomatoes that you grew in the backyard garden. As we stood there talking about the plants, a few mosquitos buzzed around us. I wondered out loud how Phoenyx would deal with this environment and told Norberto that she had lived in a large city all her life, minus the few times I took her backpacking in the American wilderness, and her global travels. Unlike most other people who visit the Amazon Rainforest to drink Ayahuasca, she chose the Andes Mountains on her first trip to Peru for the sole purpose of avoiding the mosquitos. Phoenyx was scheduled to arrive a couple days after me, so I would need to wait and see how she responded to the little flying demons.

About twenty minutes later we reached a clearing in the rainforest and I saw small buildings spread around the property. In this part of Brazil it is common to see rainforest with cattle pastures sporadically carved out of the landscape. We've all heard sad stories of South America's disappearing rainforest. I guess the good news is that the land in this region is not completely cleared, and many species of plants and animals continue to survive as they neighbor the ranchers. Norberto had purchased the land already in this condition and carried on the tradition by grazing a small herd. This style of land management gives the property a much more open feel than what would otherwise be a confined situation. It also defines a boundary between wild and potentially dangerous animals, and humans. The guest cabins are located on the edge of this boundary. On rare occasion signs of jaguar have been reported in the region. The three dogs living on the property certainly reduced our chance of ever witnessing one of these mysterious animals. I chose the cabin closest to the outdoor kitchen and dropped my backpack, but before I could rest, Norberto asked me to check the bathroom sink. I turned the faucet and nothing came out. He told me that we needed to fix the intake for the water supply system. The sun was setting fast and he had other plans for the evening, so if I wanted water for drinking, showering or flushing the toilet then we had to go now.

I met the three white dogs that we would be feeding for the next seven weeks and fortunately they had no problems with me. I was never much of a dog person, but we seemed to get along fine during our first encounter. Lukey was the father and alpha leader of the pack. Linda was the mother and Roly Poly was their son. As we went to unplug the water filter, Lukey and Roly Poly raced ahead of us to clear the path, and Linda stayed behind to offer protection. I would later learn that this was standard procedure, and the dogs were like a personal security team that wouldn't allow me to walk more than twenty meters without an escort, even when I just wanted to pee on a bush in private. It was always Lukey in front, Linda by my side and Roly Poly somewhere in between. Along the way Norberto pointed to the white temple where we would soon be drinking Ayahuasca while he was away traveling. The eight-sided building was large enough to comfortably serve about twenty people during ceremony, and sat the highest on the land. Like the path leading up to the property, the temple was also surrounded by young medicinal plants that would hopefully mature and be used for ceremony someday.

We climbed under the barbed wire fence that separates cow pasture from our living area. Norberto mentioned that he would later teach me to mend the fence for the times when the cows escape, and also how to herd the animals back into their territory. We entered the rainforest once again, but this time the path leading to the water filter was narrower than the one leading to the property. I was reminded of *Indiana Jones*, the hero I grew up watching who went on adventurous missions to exotic places. In my case, the name *Minnesota Johnson* was probably more appropriate. As I grabbed trees to pull myself up steep sections of the trail, thoughts arose of poisonous snakes and spiders, but since we were in a hurry I followed Norberto's lead and trusted that he would give me a full update when the timing was right. A few days later Phoenyx would find a poisonous snake sleeping near the dining area. When she called Norberto for guidance he immediately arrived with an axe and chopped its head off. An unfortunate day for the snake, but best for them not to live too close to the humans. When we reached the stream I was amazed to learn the filter only blocks large particles from entering the system and that we were drinking pure water without any form of treatment. The source of the stream was a spring located on his property deep in the forest, so there were no other humans to contaminate the water between here and there.

After cleaning debris from the filter we headed back down the hill for one last stop to see the outdoor kitchen. He showed me the foods he had purchased to match my restricted diet, due to allergies. With the exception of a couple solar panels and car batteries the property had no electricity, so he showed me the matches to light the candles and propane stove. I noticed a huge toad sitting in front of the stove and asked what it was. Norberto told me they are rumored to contain 5meo-DMT, which is probably the most potent psychedelic molecule on the planet, but there has not yet been any scientific confirmation. If that were true then these toads were similar to the Sonoran Desert Toads in northern Mexico and the southwestern US that have gained much attention recently in the Sacred Medicine community. Oddly enough, the dogs made no effort to eat or chase the psychedelic amphibians. I guess they were not as interested in altering their consciousness as I was. We lit a few candles and said goodbye before Norberto raced back down the trail through the dark. Well, here I am, I thought. In less than a day I went from a busy airport in Rio de Janeiro to completely alone at the very end of a bumpy dirt road in the rainforest. The nearest neighbor was about a twenty-five minute walk away. As I stood there in the candlelight I wondered what my first dinner should be and began searching for ingredients while trying not to step on the DMT toads that were patiently waiting to catch their own dinners. After preparing a simple meal of rice and eggs I sat down to eat as the first stars appeared, the fireflies began to glow, and a chorus of frogs and insects croaked and buzzed.

I walked over to the cabin and watched my personal security team go underneath the building for the night, as they would the entire time we were staying there. Despite being all alone in the middle of this foreign environment, I felt safe having these guard dogs sleeping beneath me. The bathroom was nicer than I had expected for a rustic healing center, and I enjoyed the comfort of a shower from the hot-water-on-demand, propane-powered system Norberto had installed. Finally, the day was over as I collapsed onto the mattress. The flood of new information and sensory input was nearly overwhelming, yet I was very pleased to be starting an adventure. Little did I know that day would soon be the beginning of the book you are now holding.

The next morning I awoke to a gorgeous view of the lush rainforest. Norberto had built windows on the entire wall of the cabin that directly faced the forest, to give guests the feeling of being among the plants and trees while relaxing under the protection of the roof. I spent the second day exploring the property, and getting plenty of rest while waiting for Phoenyx to arrive. On the third day she came and once again our busy shaman made a brief appearance before racing back downhill for other appointments. The look on her face was of someone trying to comprehend a radically different environment for the first time. She seemed happy to see me, but I assumed she was challenged by our new home for the next seven weeks. The land was literally alive, crawling and buzzing, a stark contrast to the sterile steel and concrete cities she was familiar with. Yes, this transition would probably take time to complete. Eventually we settled down and looked at the eight hundred milliliter Mason jar of Ayahuasca that he had left us. The idea of drinking it without his supervision in this wild place was intimidating, yet exciting. We decided to rest for a few days and adjust to our surroundings before attempting our first ceremony. And that's when things would really start to get interesting…

Death and Insanity

Before leaving the US I had anticipated having loads of free time in Brazil, so I downloaded a few movies to my iPad for entertainment. During those first few days of rest on the property, we watched an Icelandic documentary called *InnSæi* that basically argues we live in a society where the rational mind is completely out of control. Thoughts, information and data rule our lives while emotion, intuition and stillness have been reduced to forgotten and misunderstood aspects of our existence. As a result our health, happiness and environment suffer. While the film never mentioned Ayahuasca, it reminded me of the important role Sacred Medicines could play in providing a counterbalance to a world increasingly dependent on the mind. The recent emergence of Ayahuasca, at least to our culture since it has been around for millennia, provides an excellent opportunity to heal our relationships, our planet and ourselves for those who are ready and willing to take that big step.

Ayahuasca is a great mystery that I could never claim to fully understand. However, based on the expert guidance of Norberto and my personal experience over the years I would like to share my interpretation with you of how this Sacred Medicine works to improve our health. Ayahuasca is often called Madre, the Mother, due to her caring nature and tendency to give us tough love. She is also called the Doctor due to her ability to look deep inside and see exactly what it is that we need. Like a doctor who sedates a patient prior to surgery she sometimes makes the repairs without us even realizing it is happening, but often times we need to put forth some effort to fix the problem. The procedure can look something like this: first you are shown a situation in your life that is causing suffering. Next you are invited to feel the emotions associated with this situation and understand on a deep and conscious level the consequences of this situation to your health and your life. If you can accept this offer then hopefully the emotion will be quickly processed during the ceremony, but the amount of time required until completion is unknown. This process can be extremely challenging, which is why Norberto describes the Ayahuasca temple as a Divine Hospital where spiritual surgery is performed without anesthesia. According to my personal experience and authors I've read such as Doctors Gabor Maté and Joe Tafur, mental, physical and personal problems result from the storage of unprocessed thoughts and emotions that eventually become toxic to our body and mind. These toxins result in blockages that reduce the flow of energy through the system leading to pain and eventually disease. A visit to the Divine Hospital can cleanse these toxins and clear the blockages, but unfortunately, as I'm about to explain, it usually works without the anesthesia.

People often describe an Ayahuasca ceremony as years of therapy performed in one night. The advantage being that one night is obviously much faster than one year, but it can come at a very high cost. Knowing how the procedure works can make an Ayahuasca ceremony flow much more smoothly and effectively. According to Norberto there are four types of feeling: blaming others for your feelings (it's all their fault), pitying yourself for your feelings (why does this always happen to me?), attaching stories to your feelings (this happened because...) and existential feeling (simply feel, nothing more). Of these four, only existential feeling allows the feeling to pass and healing to occur. For example, during our first ceremony on the property I felt both sadness and compassion for my mother. She had been dealing with a challenging situation for a long time and couldn't seem to change it. I realized that I had been shielding myself from the discomfort of sadness, and as a result also neglected to show my compassion. I knew that for the sadness to pass I would need to fully feel and be conscious of my relationship with her. It's very tempting to push those uncomfortable emotions away, especially in that raw and vulnerable state. As a result of that experience I was determined to express my sympathy during our next communication. Here's the tricky part, if you choose to feel the emotions simply to accelerate their passing then it doesn't work. You must feel them with the sole intention of genuinely feeling them, and trust me this can be quite uncomfortable, which is exactly why we avoided them when they first entered our lives!

During our first ceremonies on the property I became aware of how my rational mind sometimes reacts to the experience: it runs away from Ayahuasca like a scared animal trying to escape a predator. It seems as if my mind gets trapped in a corner with no chance of survival, and then suddenly escapes to another corner only to be trapped again. I notice my mind slowly being consumed by the predator so I focus on something, anything, to hold onto reality. Maybe it's a cow in the pasture outside the window, or the dogs barking in the distance, whatever it takes to avoid the un-*think*-able, losing my mind to the predator. Now you may be wondering how a substance that I describe as a predator to my mind could possibly be called Madre or Doctor, but allow me to explain. There are many possible emotions we may experience during an Ayahuasca ceremony. However, according to Norberto the two most common and difficult for people to face are fear of death and fear of insanity. Why these two you ask? My understanding is that while the mind can be a powerful tool, in modern times it is used more than necessary (as described in the documentary *InnSæi*). Madre attempts to restore balance by reducing the role of the mind (death), at least during the ceremony, or confusing the mind (insanity). A reduced mind can resemble death because many people associate their mind with their identity, therefore when the mind is reduced so is the identity. Most sages would say that you are not your mind; in fact what you truly are is something much greater. I'm fully aware of this wise advice, yet when I'm sitting in ceremony and Ayahuasca seems to be on a mission to capture and consume my mind it truly feels like I'm dying, which can be terrifying. If you don't feel like you are dying then chances are good that you will think you are going insane. Again, this is Madre's attempt to tame the out of control mind that most of us suffer from these days by radically altering our perception and sense of reality. No need to worry though as she is certainly not trying to permanently harm you. On the contrary, you should notice in a few hours, days or weeks that she is enhancing your quality of life and improving your mind. Easier said than done though as it is quite common for people to freak out during a ceremony and say things like, "Call an ambulance, I'm dying!" During our first ceremony I laid on my mattress wondering, "What am I doing here?" and then swore that I would never drink again. Oddly enough I was in ceremony only five days later ready for another cup, though this time a slightly larger dose than the previous one! I guess something inside me, something beyond my mind, I call it my Higher Self, recognizes the healing quality of the medicine.

It is now clear to me at least one of the primary ways that Ayahuasca brings healing to our lives. By existentially feeling a painful emotion that we are presented with during ceremony rather than attaching blame, pity or a story to it, we can process that stored emotion, clear the stagnation and allow the energy to flow once again. If you have a strong rational mind like me then you may be wondering how many minutes you must existentially feel for since it sometimes seems like eternity. According to Norberto there is no time limit, but the sooner you existentially feel, the sooner it passes. True healing occurs when we surrender to the medicine and say to the Doctor, "Do with me as you wish," he added. This includes surrendering to death and insanity.

During our second ceremony I had been mourning the impending loss of my ego, which odd as it may sound felt like attending my own funeral. After simmering in sadness for nearly an hour I eventually decided that was enough and slowly stood up off my mattress. I struggled to put on my shoes and zigzagged out the door and across the grass down to the stream nearby. Stepping from the grass into the rainforest was like walking through a portal into another dimension and I became fascinated by my new surroundings. The sound of the rushing water ahead pulled me forward until I reached the most incredible waterfall flowing over green moss-covered rocks with a magical looking pool below. I carefully climbed the slippery rocks and listened to a tiny voice inside that beckoned me to "drink the waterfall." Like drinking water from a fire hose I gulped down the rainforest water and turned to see the three dogs burst down the path to check on me as my guard dogs always do. After staring at me curiously for a few moments we ran back to the temple together as I repeated the mantra out loud, "Holy fucking cow, holy fucking cow, holy fucking cow!" Phoenyx awaited my return and was surprised to see the joyous expression of a man who only twenty minutes earlier was reduced to loud sighs and unintelligible grunts. As cliché as it may sound, in that moment I gained a renewed appreciation for the phrase, "Nature heals." After all, what else than the grace of the rainforest could explain such an instantaneous shift in my consciousness? As I returned to the temple to lie down on my mattress, I realized that the mourning for my dying ego had suddenly passed and been replaced with a celebration for the emergence of what had been obscured by the ego. As the documentary

InnSæi had recommended, I followed my intuition, which led me to the waterfall, where suddenly the loss of my mind transformed from a tragedy into a blessing.

Breaking Good

Christmas of 2017 was certainly one of the most unusual that I have ever experienced. The cold temperatures and white snow covered yards that I typically associate with this holiday in the North were replaced with the hot weather and lush green vegetation you would expect in a rainforest twenty-two degrees south of the equator. Instead of icy roads busy with people driving to deliver gifts for the family gathering, there was a lone dirt trail leading to our isolated property that had been too eroded from years of heavy rainfall for anything larger than a horse to travel on. Instead of a Christmas tree decorated with lights and ornaments, there was a large chili pepper bush in the garden that glowed with hundreds of red fiery fruits. Despite all these major differences in weather and vegetation I still could not have predicted the ultimate reason this was going to be one of the most memorable Christmas days of my life.

The approaching date of December 25 represented more than a major international celebration, it was also the day

Norberto and his partner would leave the property to go traveling for three weeks. In the weeks leading up to Christmas we had already spent time alone while they were away on shorter trips, but this was going to be an extended period of isolation. The plan was for Phoenyx and I to be caretakers in their absence and to have ceremonies in the temple when we were not busy with our personal projects or the small amount of chores we were assigned. I had mixed thoughts on the situation; on one hand I enjoyed their presence and found his expert guidance extremely valuable. Many of the gems of wisdom found in this book come directly from conversations we had while he was here. On the other hand I looked forward to being independent because I believe an equal amount of gems are mined through the process of exploration and experimentation. During those first three weeks on the land we had only left once to visit the closest small town, which we did with the assistance of a ride in Norberto's vehicle. After he left and a ride was no longer available, the chances of us walking to town decreased even further because it was nearly a five hour round trip walk plus the possibility of intense thunderstorms or high heat, so we had made sure there were enough supplies to support us in the coming weeks. In addition to the cans of sardines, bags of tapioca and dozens of eggs he provided, I had asked if there was any possibility of getting more Ayahuasca since we already drank about half a liter, and to our delight he assured us that he would bring more medicine before leaving. Like a child eagerly waiting to receive his Christmas presents I was very curious to know how different the next batch would be from what we currently had. I practiced being patient since I knew how busy he often was, but on the day before their flight I became worried that Santa had forgotten to bring our gift this year and knew that it was time to ask.

After Phoenyx gently repeated our request for more medicine Norberto replied, "Yes, there is some here in the kitchen I will give you, and I can add a little booster to make it stronger." He then asked us, "Have you ever heard of Jurema?" It took several days for me to fully understand the implications of that simple question. I had not heard of Jurema and assumed that it must be a different type of vine than the Ourinho (the little golden) Ayahuasca we were drinking, which I soon learned it was not. He explained that it is a powder from the root bark of a plant that grows in northern Brazil, scientifically classified as *Mimosa Tenuiflora*. To properly explain how Jurema works you need a basic understanding of how Ayahuasca works. The Ayahuasca medicinal brew in its most basic form is a blend of wood from the Ayahuasca vine and leaves from the Chacruna shrub, which are scientifically classified as *Banisteriopsis caapi* and *Psychotria viridis* respectively. Chacruna leaves contain Dimethyltryptamine (DMT), which is one of the primary chemicals of Ayahuasca that alters consciousness. DMT is not orally active since the monoamine oxidase enzymes in our stomach rapidly degrade it before the effects are felt. Wood from the Ayahuasca vine contains monoamine oxidase inhibitors (MAOI) that prevent the enzymes from degrading the DMT and allow us to consume it orally. Amazon natives understood these complex biochemical reactions centuries if not millennia before modern scientists finally began to understand how Ayahuasca works in the human body. However, when it comes to Jurema, the mystery continues. Scientists know that Jurema root bark contains DMT, but they have not yet detected any MAOIs, and as a result the plant should not be orally active. Despite this, some natives of Brazil have discovered that when the plant is consumed orally and not mixed with any other plants, they are still able to experience the effects of DMT. Apparently some of these natives have also been introduced to the idea of combining their medicine with Ayahuasca. Now imagine a plant loaded with DMT that is already orally active, and combine that with an MAOI to extend the duration and intensity of the experience. Norberto was proposing that we too see what happens when these powerful plants come together, and if that wasn't already more than enough he added that, "Jurema is used to enter the spirit world."

After receiving this totally unexpected introduction to Jurema, Norberto began searching among the numerous unlabeled jars and bottles of dried herbs and liquids on the shelves. "Here is four hundred milliliters of some older Ayahuasca," he exclaimed as he grabbed a couple small bottles that were sitting next to the olive oil bottles. "We can boost these with the Jurema," he said as he put a pot on the stove. He started the process and then asked if I would be willing to help by continuously stirring the brew while keeping the heat just below a simmer to prevent burning. I was definitely willing to help, in fact while planning for the trip I had told Phoenyx how much I would love to participate in the medicine making process, which is known here as the Feitio. Well, without any warning I suddenly got what I asked for, though it wasn't quite how I expected, as is often the case with Sacred Medicine. Every time I walked from our cabin to the outdoor kitchen, I was reminded of my desire to learn the process because the Feitio was built in between the two building (the term Feitio refers not only to making the medicine, but also the structure where the making occurs). The Feitio in this case was a roof supported by several wooden posts that gave shelter to a large earthen stove capable of heating multiple fifty-liter stainless steel pots. For now I would be happy stirring the small one-liter pot, and who knows, perhaps I would scale up and experience the full Feitio some other time?

As I slowly stirred the brew, Norberto continued searching among the jars and bottles until he exclaimed, "I found a couple more bottles," which I guessed must have been leftovers from a previous healing retreat. The bottles hissed when he loosened the caps and he told us they had fermented, but with a light simmer we could vaporize the alcohol content and kill any bacteria living inside. "With these bottles we will make a different batch," he said, and then instructed me to harvest a bowl of Chacruna leaves from the forest. The day before I had been given a tour of the medicine plants growing in the forest in preparation for the Chacruna that we agreed to plant while he and his partner were away, so I knew where to find the plants. Norberto explained how the Chacruna is sometimes called Rainha and the Ayahuasca is called Rei, meaning the two plants together become the queen and king of the rainforest. I grabbed Phoenyx for the task and we entered the forest through a thin path behind the cabins. Mosquitos buzzed around us as I pointed to the Ayahuasca vines reaching for the sun and warned her not to step on them. When you first arrive on the property everything is green and all the plants look the same, but with practice you begin to distinguish between the wild plants and the cultivated medicine hidden throughout the forest. We picked until the bowl was nearly full then headed back to the kitchen. During the forest tour Norberto had taught me that the oldest leaves contained the most DMT and could be identified by the torn leaves and light mold that grew on the surface. Back in the kitchen I told him that we picked the worst leaves we could find and he replied with a huge smile, "Well done, the worst leaves are the best kind!" We rinsed and shredded the fresh picked Chacruna leaves into small pieces and then added them to the old fermented Ayahuasca that had been found on the shelf earlier.

The first batch had simmered and stirred for a couple hours and was now ready to be filtered. We learned to filter as much Jurema powder out of the brew as possible because while Jurema is a purgative to begin with, the excess powder can make people feel even more nauseous when they drink it. To be conservative the filtered powder from the first batch was then added to the second batch so more medicine could be extracted. This process can be repeated multiple times until there is little medicine remaining in the powder, and then the separated batches of brew can be combined and reduced through evaporation at a low temperature.

Have you ever heard a cook say the meal they prepared was made with love? It turns out there may be more truth to that saying than you realize. The practice of talking, singing, praying or sending positive energy to the medicine during the Feitio is known as inscribing. Norberto claims this step of the process is crucial and can literally determine the outcome of an experience for the people who drink it, so we were encouraged to inscribe our medicine as we stirred. In addition, he offered us a tiny serving of medicine from the first batch to introduce the spirit of the plant to our bodies and be more focused during the Feitio. Later on I discovered that Phoenyx chose to sing *Ordinary Human* by OneRepublic while she stirred, when I walked into the kitchen and heard, "There will be peace in the city tonight..." During my turn at stirring I immediately knew that I wanted to feel the vibrations of Phish during the next ceremony and started singing their song *Rise*, "We've got to riiiiiise up, and come together, come together, come together..." Naturally, the name of the second batch had to be Phish Republic, so on December 25, 2017, our first creation came into existence, born of second wash Jurema powder, fresh-picked moldy Chacruna leaves and leftover fermented Ayahuasca. We could hardly wait to test this new brew, or as OneRepublic says, "I'm just an ordinary human, sometimes I medicate..."

I sometimes use movies and music to interpret the Sacred Medicine journeys I have and put them into a better perspective. While I quit watching TV many years ago, I still occasionally rent or stream a series that catches my attention. One such series is *Breaking Bad*, which I was curious about because the show takes place in Albuquerque, New Mexico, where I had once lived for a year. I decided to watch the first season to understand why the show was receiving so much attention. The main character is a high school chemistry teacher who receives a cancer diagnosis, and then begins producing methamphetamine under the alias Heisenberg to pay the high costs of health care in the US. Later that night Phoenyx and I laughed as we made jokes about the unexpected kitchen lesson, and compared Norberto to Heisenberg who sometimes uses the phrase "let's cook" when it's times to make a new batch of methamphetamine. Both of these unorthodox men are extremely proud of the high quality psychoactive drugs they create; they both practice their craft as a means of supporting their family, and as we saw in the kitchen that day they improvise when necessary to get the job done. But that is where the similarities end; they are obviously heading in opposite directions. *Breaking Bad* is a slang term for a person who goes to the dark side, loses their way and engages in morally wrong or illegal behavior. The title describes how an ordinary human can rise through the ranks of producer, distributor, and eventually murderer and cartel leader. On the other hand Norberto is like the anti-Heisenberg of an emerging hit TV show called Breaking Good who goes to the light side, finds his way and engages in morally right or legal behavior (at least in Brazil it is). Heisenberg is a formally trained chemist who uses lab equipment to precisely measure chemicals and blend them together to produce toxic substances that desperate people use for escape. Our anti-Heisenberg is a traditionally trained herbalist who uses kitchen utensils and approximation to produce detoxifying medicines that desperate people use for healing. Heisenberg exploits addicts and keeps people asleep, which does nothing to improve the world. Our anti-Heisenberg helps people end their addictions and awaken their consciousness, which I believe is what the world needs most right now.

We created enough medicine that day to explore the spirit world many times during their absence. Because of this we were satisfied, but still a little apprehensive about being left alone with a medicine we had never tried before. Up until that point the only guidance we had received was an approximation of the size of our dose, to stay focused, and that the negative spirits have as much to teach us as the positive kind. Many questions remained before they left to catch a flight, such as how long does it take to feel the effects, or how does one best navigate the spirit world? However, there would be no time to answer as a thunderstorm rumbled in the distance. Norberto suddenly announced his departure and explained that during a big storm the river flows over the bridge on the road leading to the property, and it becomes too dangerous, if not impossible to cross. They needed to leave now or risk being stranded on the property and missing their flight.

This is crazy, we thought. What kind of person leaves two people with arguably one of the strongest Sacred Medicines on planet Earth, and for their first experience tells them nothing more than to stay focused?! Then we realized the kind of person that does that is the kind that trusts our ability to handle challenging situations, and up until that point we had never been given a reason to doubt him, so why worry? In fact, we eventually viewed the situation as a compliment considering many people simply could not handle drinking Jurema with or without a shaman present. Let's not forget that Phoenyx had been working with him for a year as an assistant, and many years as a participant, so he clearly knew what she was capable of. Norberto can be a bit wild at times, as you would expect a man to be coming from such a wild place. In all honesty though, I never suspected that he would put us or any of the participants that depend on him for guidance in harm's way. His relaxed style is actually very refreshing in comparison to the US culture, which is drowning in fear, worry and anxiety. Evidence of this can be seen where you can't walk more than a few steps without seeing insurance for this, disclaimers for that, and warnings all around. Yes, snakes and spiders live here, don't touch them. Yes, you may encounter negative spirits, stay focused. Life in the rainforest, or anywhere in the world, has threats, but there is no need to obsess over them.

In retrospect it's difficult to say whether he forgot to bring us a new bottle of Ayahuasca along with the hundred other things he needed to do before getting on an international flight, or he simply planned all along to cook some Jurema for us. Either way, Santa delivered what we asked for, strong medicine to last through the coming weeks, and a Christmas story I will never forget.

Introduction to Jurema

The day began like any other; I awoke to the sunrise and stared out the window at the lush green view. My first thought was, today is ceremony day, and I felt a mix of excited anticipation and fear of the unknown. You need to understand that it was not an ordinary ceremony day, it was the first time we would drink the potent Sacred Medicine called Jurema. Before ceremony could begin though, Phoenyx and I would need to complete our morning routine of feeding the chickens, feeding the dogs and of course feeding ourselves. There was one more addition to our list of morning chores that would later prove to be an important factor in the confusing day that awaited us, we also needed to receive an order of supplies scheduled to arrive that day.

Following the morning feeding we returned to the cabin to pack our bags for a day in the temple. I completed my preparation and as usual lay down on the bed while a wave of nervous tiredness washed over my body. It is probably my mind's way of reacting to an impending annihilation resulting from the powerful psychedelic that we would soon be drinking. The word *annihilate* sounds quite threatening, but in this context it refers to the destruction of that which is no longer needed. In the big picture I welcome the benefits that come from an annihilation with open arms, but in the moment it can be slightly intimidating. Anyway, as I nearly drifted off into an afternoon siesta the sound of aggressive barking startled me out of bed. Our loyal guard dogs announced the arrival of the supplies and I looked out the window down the hill to see two men on horseback surrounded by many other horses. They navigated through the gates of the property and began moving uphill. I knew what was coming next; it wouldn't be long before Lukey the alpha dog began to loudly defend his territory. I quickly put on some clothes and rushed out the door to try and intercept him from greeting the horsemen. The mounted riders climbed the hill to the outdoor kitchen and left the other horses behind while I successfully leashed Lukey just in time. The deliveryman rapidly spoke in a Portuguese dialect, but I could only simply reply that I speak English. My lack of Portuguese had not been a problem up until now as we rarely saw another human on the isolated property, but as you will soon discover, it would have been useful that day. Instead I improvised with some hand gestures and basic Spanish, which was enough to receive a heavy order of propane gas and dog food. After finishing the fresh banana and water we had offered them, one of the horsemen did something I couldn't understand. Prior to leaving he asked for rope to close the gate that is meant to protect the kitchen and garden area in case the cows escape from the fenced pasture. Due to our communication gap I was confused about why he insisted on closing that gate since the cows were clearly grazing in the high pasture, but accepted his offer. I then unleashed Lukey when they were far enough away.

My attention soon shifted from the strange request of the horseman to the task at hand, ceremony day. However, this was no ordinary ceremony. It had already been intimidating enough to drink Ayahuasca without the presence of a shaman, but at least we had drunk that medicine with him before. Today we would drink a new plant that we had never experienced before, with or without a shaman present, so we were extra careful in our preparation ritual. The process occurred as usual by unpacking our bags in the temple and arranging the essential items, like Phoenyx's *Iron Man* action figure for protection, an iPad for music since neither of us were musicians, glasses of water, citronella spray for mosquitos and flashlights for after sunset. We set the altar with a large candle and a pitcher of water meant to attract and capture negative energies. There were paper towels and purge buckets near our mattresses in case of emergency, though instead of using them we preferred to walk outside and release into the grass. With practice I find it easier to anticipate when the vomit is coming and rarely need the bucket. Some people do struggle to walk when the medicine is strong, so it's nice for them to have that option available. There is no shame in purging inside the temple during ceremony, in fact the release should be celebrated, but if you have the ability to step outside or visit the toilet, then why not? Phoenyx was facing a common fear and checked our mattresses for any hidden giant spiders. Everything was neat, orderly and symmetrical, as you might expect from a US military veteran and a former German police officer. We took great care in preparing for ceremony partly because Norberto had advised us that as long as we show respect for the ceremony, the temple, the medicine and each other then we need not fear drinking in his absence. Also included in our ritual was an Amazonian wood called Palo Santo that was burned like incense and used to smudge ourselves and the temple of any negative energies. We anointed ourselves with oil prepared for this exact purpose that had been purchased earlier in Glastonbury, England. As always, we said the opening prayer and shared our intentions while drawing a card from the tarot deck. Shortly after we were swallowing the Ayahuasca and Jurema hybrid (Juremuasca) that we had created, which unfortunately tasted no better than Ayahuasca, but not worse either.

Other than trying a super potent medicine for the first time without the assistance of a shaman, and receiving a delivery from the horsemen, ceremony day was flowing as it usually does. I lay on my back and began my typical yawning. As my mind became increasingly aware of what was happening, I wondered how many more minutes before it was dissolved and overcome by an occupying plant spirit. Nearly two hours later and the wondering continued; should we have drunk more? The last thing I want to do is top up my dose a few minutes before a tsunami washes over me and have an overly intense experience. As we considered how much booster to have, Phoenyx looked out the window and commented on the horse in the pasture. "No," I said, "the neighbor took the lone horse away weeks ago, it must be a cow." She replied, "Either I'm tripping and seeing a unicorn, or there is a horse near the temple." "In fact," she said upon walking over to the window for a closer look, "there are six of them!"

I couldn't believe this observation because other than the fourteen cows living on the property there were no animals that could be mistaken for a horse, but when our loyal guard dogs started barking loudly I knew these horses were something more than a strong DMT vision. The medicine was coming on as I struggled to make sense of this confusing scene. Suddenly it dawned on me, the horsemen had multiple horses with them when they first arrived to make their delivery. Had they also delivered horses to feed on the pasture? Were they trying to explain this to me in Portuguese? Was that what he meant when he held up six fingers? Was this why he requested rope to close the garden gate? If so, then why were the horses on the human side of the barbed wire fence and not the cow side? Norberto had told us to expect a delivery of propane gas and dog food, so why did this normally thoughtful man neglect to mention the horses? Most importantly, why was this happening two hours after I drank Juremuasca for the first time in my life?

I realized that my altered mind needed to shift gears from questions to solutions mode. The dogs were barking and I tried repeatedly to call them off but knew this was a futile attempt as they regularly barked anytime the cows came near the living area. At least the cows can go to higher pastures when the dogs bark, but since the horses were on our side of the fence there was no place for them to escape, and I knew the barking would be relentless as the dogs *defended* the property. Or maybe they were herding; whatever they were doing it was annoying, and four more hours of constant barking was no way to experience ceremony. Action was necessary, so we decided to text Norberto for guidance. How fortunate we were that a few days before departing for a three-week journey he had satellite Internet installed on this remote rainforest property. I never expected to be sending text messages during a Juremuasca ceremony, and certainly not to a shaman since I always assumed we would be drinking in his presence. I guess that's the era we live in, with instant access to a digital shaman. Rather than waiting for a reply we decided to leash the alpha dog once again and rope off access to the temple area so the horses couldn't eat the precious Ayahuasca and Chacruna plants that were growing all around us.

Thank God we cautiously underdosed during our first attempt at drinking this powerful medicine and were able to restore peace, at least temporarily. I would rate our experience as a "plus two" on the Shulgin scale. Sasha Shulgin was a psychopharmacologist and chemist who self-tested hundreds of psychedelic chemicals that he created in the laboratory at his home in California. He defines a plus two experience as one when the drug's effects may be "repressible and made secondary to other chosen activities." Phoenyx discovered during her time as an assistant that Ayahuasca allows a seasoned participant the ability to complete an important task when focus is necessary. That is assuming she doesn't drink a "plus three" dose, which Shulgin defines as one where "ignoring the action of a drug is no longer an option." Plus two or not, I still think we deserve some credit for making calm and clear decisions under the influence of such a mind-altering substance. We obviously would have never started ceremony had we known there were six horses wandering around the living area of the property, but now that the situation seemed to be under control it was time for a booster shot of Juremuasca. We doubled our dose and waited for the show to begin, not yet realizing it had already begun hours before when the horsemen first arrived. My expectations of entering the spirit world never fully manifested that day, which reminded me it's not a good idea to have expectations. Actually there were some brief beautiful visions and sounds, but it was mostly a dark experience with all sorts of worms and creepy crawling insects occupying my view. Oddly enough Phoenyx had the same dark insect filled experience. Was this a case of telepathy? After all, the chemical Harmaline found in Ayahuasca was initially given the name Telepathine. Or were dark visions of insects simply a typical experience for people drinking this plant? We later learned from Norberto that the type of Black Ayahuasca used to brew the Juremuasca was more likely to have caused the insect visions than the Jurema. Meanwhile, back in the physical realm the peace was short lasting as Lukey nearly choked himself to death on the leash while attempting to bark anytime the horses were within smelling distance, and the other two followed his lead. Eventually the sun went down and visions of spirit insects were replaced by material insects as mosquitos, cockroaches, ants and fireflies buzzed and crawled around us. Big sigh... we had more than enough for one day and decided it was time to close ceremony before heading back to the cabin.

Besides the insects, I think the only entity we met in the spirit world that day was Loki, the trickster god of Norse mythology. It must have been Loki who let loose the six horses, a situation that would have been challenging even while sober. We closed our eyes and pictured how his smiling face looks after successfully deceiving *Thor*. And it was probably he who removed the toilet paper from the outdoor composting toilet stall when I needed it most during ceremony. I had reached the stall in a state of digestive distress only to discover the toilet paper was missing from the normal spot. I considered running back to the temple for more, but this was an emergency and it was time to have a seat. After finishing my business I considered grabbing a leaf but feared in my altered state I might accidentally grab a thorny leaf, or a toad instead. So I pulled up my white ceremonial pants half way and stumbled back to the temple with my dirty bottom hanging out. I entered the temple and Phoenyx told me there was paper, in the second stall, so I gracefully backed out, rear end first. As I walked across the lawn once again I finally realized it was probably not Loki, but Norberto's partner who moved the paper. I heard her singing Bollywood tunes at the temple a few days before they departed, so I guess she prefers the rainforest view offered by the more exposed stall on the left.

Anyway, the digital shaman replied to my text and the next morning the horses were removed from the property. I unleashed the alpha dog and he chased the cows to celebrate his new freedom. Later that day a lightning strike terrified me with a deafening crack a mere hundred meters away, and I understood that the challenges never cease here in the rainforest. Apparently before I am rewarded with higher vibration and heavenly visions I first need to deal with the worms, horses, dogs and poop down here on planet Earth.

An important lesson that people in the spiritual community often fail to learn. I think this quote by Carl Jung is most appropriate for my Juremuasca initiation, "No tree, it is said, can grow to heaven unless its roots reach down to hell." The hell part is not always easy or fun, but it is probably necessary before we can enjoy the view from the mystical heights.

The Hierophant

Our second Juremuasca ceremony had all the necessary ingredients to qualify as an epic experience. In fact, I would even go so far as to describe it as beyond epic, at least from my perspective it was, but I'll let you be the judge of that. To begin with we had chosen January 1 as the date of the ceremony to celebrate the New Year in a memorable way. You may wonder why we didn't choose December 31 instead since this date is typically known for festivities and reflections of the old year, but our decision was strongly influenced by the arrival of a full moon on January 1. Besides, I like the idea of looking forward and starting the first day of the new year in style.

A couple weeks before I did an Internet search for the exact time and date of the full moon so we could plan our ceremony accordingly. To my surprise I discovered that the first full moon of the year is known as the Wolf Moon. Besides simply being a cool name it was also relevant to us considering our primary reason for staying on the property was to feed and watch the three dogs living there. Like I said, I never really liked dogs very much, so the idea of volunteering to watch three dogs for several weeks may seem a little strange. I've always been sound sensitive, so it was mostly the frequent barking of the neighbors' dogs that drove me crazy. I like cats; cats are much more peaceful than dogs. To be fair to the dogs though, a neglectful owner is often the real problem, especially when they don't properly train their pets or ensure they are getting enough exercise. Anyway, I digress. During our first ceremony on the property I had a sudden realization that these three dogs behaved more like wolves than any I had previously known. As an outdoor enthusiast, wolves have always been a symbol for me of the last remaining wild places in the world. After decades of conflict between wolves and ranchers, the US wolf population had reached critical levels. Fortunately the Endangered Species Act intervened before it was too late, and the wolves continue to run free, at least as long as we allow them to. By making the connection between my appreciation for wolves and recognizing that our three dogs are obviously descendants of wolf ancestors, I found it difficult not to bond with them. They guarded us, slept under our cabin at night and escorted us everywhere we went as if we were part of their family. Thus my new nickname for them became the wolf pack, and the name of the coming Wolf Moon sounded especially auspicious to my ears.

So the pieces were beginning to fall into place as Phoenyx and I planned to usher in the New Year under the light of the Wolf Moon. To make things more interesting we hoped to have a more powerful experience with the Juremuasca than we did during our introduction to the new medicine. We had been standing at the gates ready to enter, but apparently did not take the threshold dose required to attend the main event. If you want to truly understand how a medicine works you can't dabble with small doses, so this time we would drink more and hopefully not be distracted by horses. We were really curious to know what a journey to the spirit world would be like, but first we performed our ceremonial rituals.

One of the ceremonial rituals that I was really beginning to enjoy was to state an intention and then draw a card from the *Aleister Crowley Thoth Tarot* deck. The tarot was relatively new to me and being the rational-minded guy that I am my first impression of it was that only airy-fairy, love and light types are attracted to this sort of thing. However, the more I learned about the meaning of the different cards the more I began to appreciate it. Each of the twenty-two trumps of the Major Arcana that we were drawing from represented an archetype, such as the Magician, Hermit or Sun. The role of archetypes in our lives was introduced by psychologist Carl Jung, and later on by scholar Joseph Campbell, who focused on the Hero archetype that is present in many myths, books and movies across all cultures on Earth. Perhaps the card I drew would somehow influence my subconscious. Could the card be an indication of the direction the ceremony would go? Whether the tarot was simply a fun addition to our ritual, or it had a deeper purpose, it became a habit that I looked forward to. During our last ceremony Phoenyx and I both drew the Hierophant, which is the archetype of a Priest. The name is derived from Greek words meaning, "To show the sacred." Not only was it a nice coincidence to draw the same card, but according to the instruction booklet we were using, Aleister Crowley says of the Hierophant, "Offer thyself Virgin to the Knowledge and Conversation of thine Holy Guardian Angel. All else is a trap." This had seemed like a very appropriate card to draw before drinking a medicine known to bring people to the spirit world. It also matched very well with the advice of Norberto to neither engage nor ignore any spirits we encountered. I never did meet my Holy Guardian Angel during the previous ceremony. Instead we met... worms. Well, maybe my Holy Guardian Angel is a worm, but it didn't feel right, so I doubt it.

The last Juremuasca ceremony felt incomplete because of the interruption from the dogs barking at the horses. For our second attempt I seriously considered recycling our Hierophant cards instead of drawing again since they appeared to be perfect for the occasion. Upon further thought we came to the conclusion that a new ceremony requires a new draw no matter how relevant and unfinished the last draw appeared. After stating her intention and sufficiently shuffling the deck Phoenyx turned over her card: the Hierophant once again. We looked at each other in disbelief for a few moments and then she handed the deck to me. I stated my intentions for the ceremony and shuffled and shuffled and shuffled as I always do, perhaps even a bit excessively, and then flipped the card. Hierophant! Now I know we live in a society where logic and science rule, but would you merely classify this event as a random coincidence, or statistical phenomenon? Synchronicities are not very easy to describe and they are even more difficult to prove, but let's take a moment to analyze the situation. From a statistical perspective the odds of repeating the first card three consecutive times in a deck of twenty-two cards is 1 out of 10,648. These are certainly not impossible odds, yet they are not very likely to happen either. I don't know exactly what it means, but it left me feeling like we weren't alone in that temple. It felt like there was a higher intelligence involved or perhaps it was a message from beyond seeking our attention. The message seemed to say that the Hierophant has meaning whether or not we knew what the meaning is. I interpreted this as yet another auspicious sign of where the night was heading and wondered what could possibly happen next.

The first few ceremonies had been challenging. Between drinking medicine without the assistance of a shaman for our first time, purging and processing some uncomfortable emotions, being introduced to new strains of Ayahuasca (Ourinho) and entirely new medicines (Jurema), so far it felt like we were recruits going through spiritual boot camp. Somewhere along the way I mentioned how great it would be if we were rewarded with a mystical experience for all our hard work to date. I joked that we didn't necessarily need to see visions of rainbows, but a lighter and higher vibrating ceremony sure would be appreciated. Shortly after drinking the booster I got exactly that. During a short walk down to the nearby waterfall we suddenly saw a rainbow uphill from the temple, and above that was a less bright second rainbow. No, not a psychedelic hallucination of a rainbow, but an actual rainbow, in fact I have an iPhone photo to prove it. I know, I know, I'm setting a bad example here, ceremonies are meant for deep introspection, not to play with our electronic devices, but there are exceptions to every rule.

Give me some credit; at least I didn't take a selfie. After all, it was the first rainbow, let alone double rainbow, we had ever seen on the property and it occurred during a Juremuasca Full Moon New Year's Eve ceremony. Phoenyx exclaimed that it was an auspicious sign, and that a Nepalese shaman had once told her that seeing one during ceremony means the spirits approve of what you are doing. The list of auspicious signs that we witnessed that day was getting longer by the minute, and the peak had not even begun.

My rainbow enthusiasm quickly passed as the first wave of Juremuasca washed over me. I rushed back inside to my mattress and laid down in preparation for the unknown. Earlier I had mentioned how people often struggle with a fear of death or insanity during ceremony. I had been improving my ability to stay calm and surrender to the medicine while an occupying spirit consumed my mind. I might even dare to say that I was beginning to slightly enjoy the transition, at least the part when the mind is gone and the Higher Self emerges. There was a distorted noise inside my head that ascended in volume and frequency, like half digital and half biological, that I looked forward to hearing as the DMT took effect. The medicine was coming on strong and I looked out the window to see the hillside covered in giant slithering snakes. That was a bit more than I could deal with so I closed my eyes and tried to relax. My right arm had been occasionally flopping up and down, and my legs twitched back and forth. The best way to describe the experience is a scene from one of those nature shows where the predator has caught the prey and the prey kicks a few times before it dies. There is no chance of escape but the animal still has involuntary reactions as it is eaten alive.

As horrible as that may sound I did my best to accept the situation and tried not to resist. When I consciously made the choice not to fight the Juremuasca a vision flashed across the back of my closed eyes. It was a blood splatter quite similar to what you would see on *Dexter*, the TV show about the Miami Police Department forensic analyst who is also a serial killer of other killers who have slipped through the legal system unpunished. Jesus, I thought, that was violent. Then I reminded myself that the blood probably came from an obsolete part of my mind that needed to go. Perhaps some useless social conditioning or limiting self-beliefs that Ayahuasca alone had not yet annihilated. Shortly after, the intensity subsided and I felt relief at having survived Juremuasca. Or not, depending on how you look at it.

Experiencing a ceremony can be like riding a roller coaster from highs to lows, and heavy to light. One such light moment occurred after surviving the initial wave of intensity that washed over me. Swallows make their homes underneath the roof of the temple and occasionally they enter through the open windows. Two of them flew in and were then circling the room trying to get out. One bird repeatedly attempted to fly through the closed upper windows instead of the open lower windows, so I said out loud, "You need to fly lower to leave the temple." And immediately after the bird did exactly that. I'm not claiming to communicate with birds, but one has to admit the timing of this was peculiar. To take it one step further the second bird became tired from trying to escape and decided to perch on a ledge for some rest. Phoenyx slowly approached the bird and calmly told it that she was there to help while extending her hands and carefully grabbing it. The bird was tired but must have been more than capable to resist her and fly away, yet it did not. The swallow screeched a few times like a little dinosaur, but never bit her while she walked over to the window and released it. Catching a wild animal with your bare hands is certainly not a normal activity, and at the same time it would be an exaggeration to call it a miracle. A couple days later while walking through the forest to clean the water filter I encountered a green lizard. I was feeling relaxed during the afterglow phase, and my mind had not fully returned. I easily picked up the little animal, and thinking that maybe it was naturally slow opened my hand. To my surprise it darted away at lightning speed. These kinds of experiences can be quite common during a ceremony and exactly what they mean is unclear to me, but after such events accumulate one after another throughout the day, it leaves me wondering if life really is as we believe it to be.

In a society increasingly disconnected from nature the significance of a full moon can easily be lost or dismissed. For Phoenyx and I the full moon serves as an important reminder in a multitude of ways. We first met at a full moon Huachuma (San Pedro cactus) celebration in a small town located in the Andes Mountains of Peru, so the full moon represents our first time coming together. In addition, the full moon represents the cycles of nature, which are increasingly being ignored due to the modern mind's linear style of thinking. Our dependence on technology drives this shift from cyclical to linear, and explains why we expect to eat out-of-season strawberries in winter, and to enjoy frosty cool homes during summer. Another example is light pollution that is bright enough in some cities to make the stars invisible. Fortunately for us though, light pollution definitely is not a problem on the very isolated property we were caring for. Later that night I gathered the strength to go outside and pee. It was now dark and my task was immediately distracted by the large glowing orb rising above the hill. A full moon is beautiful regardless of what state of mind I'm in, but under the influence of Juremuasca it was absolutely stunning, and I felt truly blessed to actually be able to see it. Summer time in Brazil means high heat and sometimes heavy rains. It had been raining regularly the prior week and I didn't expect to see the moon that night, especially since it had been raining only a few hours earlier, which of course was one of the necessary ingredients for the rainbow we witnessed. The dogs were excited and seemed to be staring at the moon as if they knew it was named for their wolf ancestors. "It's your moon, wolf pack," I said repeatedly and waited for them to hoowwwllll in response. Unfortunately they never did howl, but the bright pulse of Sirius more than compensated for their quiet mood. Sirius, also known as the Dog Star, was competing with the moon for my attention that night and I Siriusly wondered whether it was communicating with me from light years away as some claim it does. With the risk of sounding like a lunatic I must admit to feeling extremely sensitive that night to moon energy, like it was overwhelming my nervous system. I'm not the kind of guy who normally would say something like that, but after staring at the sky it felt very necessary to race back inside and use the temple roof as a shield for protection. A few hours later the intensity decreased, and we ended the night by eating outside under the stars while listening to Jason Mraz serenade the moon in his song *Bella Luna*; no candles were needed.

The fresh start to a new year, a Wolf Full Moon, four consecutive Hierophants, a rainbow, bare-handed bird catching, clear skies, a pulsating Dog Star and some very strong medicine in a temple on an isolated piece of land in the Brazilian rainforest; it doesn't get much more auspicious than that. I began this chapter by describing the ceremony as "beyond epic" and have no idea whether or not your sober rational mind will agree because it's one of those things where you really need to be there to understand the significance of it all. It's not easy putting these mystical highs into words. All I can say is that they feel epic, they feel important and they have a deeper meaning than is experienced during ordinary waking life. That must be one of the primary benefits of Sacred Medicines, to remind us how amazing life is, especially those of us who are living in poor conditions or depressing situations. They are the great interrupters that shake us out of patterns. They can drop our jaws in wonder, inspire us and show us a world we've never seen before, even when we've seen it a hundred times. Synchronicities and auspicious signs are not easy to explain and may be interpreted differently, ignored or even go unnoticed depending on the observer. For me they were directly related to my intention of the day, which was also my goal for the entire year. My resolution for 2018 was to successfully write, publish and sell a book that people both want and need. I interpreted the signs and synchronicities as: encouragement to keep moving forward; to rise above my fears and doubts about writing; that I had chosen a topic for a book that an audience would be interested in; most importantly, that I would be supported along the way by powers greater than me. So if you are reading this now then I guess the auspicious signs were more than mere coincidence, and the forces around and inside me conspired to make it happen.

***An interesting note regarding the four consecutive Hierophant cards: Several months later I discovered that the card represents not only a priest, but more specifically the High Priest of the Eleusinian Mysteries. The Mysteries were a ceremonial event that occurred for centuries in ancient Greece. During these ceremonies a beverage known as Kykeon, that is believed to have contained psychedelic ingredients, played a central role as a sacrament. To my ears, somebody who "shows the sacred" to the participants by serving them a psychedelic beverage is better described by the title of Shaman. So why were we repeatedly shown the Shaman card?

☿

Grateful Dead

"Such a long long time to be gone
And a short time to be there"

-Box of Rain, by Grateful Dead

I've always feared death. I can still remember lying in my bed at night as a little boy and crying after first becoming aware of the reality that someday I will die. Even though I didn't listen to the band until later, the lyrics above summarize my perception at the time of what would happen when my body died, and I found this thought to be very disturbing. Since then I've come to hear other interpretations of what happens at the end of life, but back then that was all I knew. It's a challenge that has confronted nearly all humans throughout history, except perhaps the religious who find comfort in the belief that they will ascend to heaven or reincarnate. My grandmother was Lutheran but I never went to church so these ideas would not bring me relief. Over the years I dealt with this fear by simply avoiding the thought. There are so many other things to think about and do, so why occupy my time with what seemed like a sad fact of life? It probably played a role in my disciplined approach to health and diet, like maybe I could drink carrot juice until immortality, or at least delay the inevitable. But as any seasoned consumer of Sacred Medicines knows, if you want to avoid the topic of death then psychedelics are the last thing you should be doing. Death is a very common theme for many people's psychedelic experiences. Psychedelics tend to dissolve our illusions and show us the world as it is, especially the areas we have been trying to avoid. For me death would occasionally make an appearance during ceremony in the form of thoughts that would surface. This was never a dramatic scary encounter because as much as psychedelics excel at confronting us directly, I find that it is still possible to avoid and look away if I choose, at least on lower doses, which brings me to this next story.

Following our introduction to Juremuasca and then the epic Wolf Full Moon New Year's celebration, Phoenyx and I felt warmed up and were ready to go a little deeper. We upped the dose and drank the Jurema thirty minutes after the Ourinho, then laid down and impatiently waited for the medicine to slowly come on. Around thirty minutes later a wave of beautiful light visions flooded my view, but since the Ourinho typically took a hundred minutes to activate I knew this was only the opening act and the main event had not begun. When the Ayahuasca MAOI base layer was finally activated the Jurema came on in full force and my eyes bulged wide open as I strained to take in all the information flowing through me. My third eye must have opened since it felt like seeing the world as a newborn for the first time. This was all still manageable, but the medicine continued to increase in strength until I didn't know what to do anymore. Of course there is nothing to *do*, but there are moments when just lying there feels uncomfortable and purging doesn't bring relief, so how to be in that intensity? To simply exist felt like a monumental task. There was a strong pull of my spirit away from my body, like an irresistible force, and while it was not necessarily attractive it was not scary either. In fact, I felt slightly curious to know where I was going. Eventually it became apparent that I was dying, or so I thought. Yes, today is the day I die in this healing temple, on this vibrant land, drinking this beautiful medicine with a woman who cares for me by my side. That actually doesn't sound too terrible. I'm still relatively young, but what better way to go? Not the kind of reaction you would expect from a guy who is afraid of death.

Let's take a short detour here to discuss the name of legendary pioneering psychedelic band Grateful Dead. They were partly responsible for my introduction to psychedelics as a young man, back when I didn't know the difference between recreational and medicinal use. After a few years of experimentation during my late teens I would eventually join the military in search of direction, college money and international travel. My recreational use of psychedelics came to nearly a complete stop, minus the occasional low dose mushroom trips, yet Grateful Dead always remained on my playlist, among other bands representing the counterculture. My psychedelic fast lasted approximately fifteen years until I began hearing guests on Joe Rogan's podcast describing Ayahuasca. Anyway, the story goes that the band borrowed their name from a random entry in a dictionary. According to *Encyclopedia Britannica,* the Grateful Dead motif comes from folktales about "the spirit of a deceased person who bestows benefits on the one responsible for his burial." Quite a fitting definition for what was to come for me on Norberto's land.

Now back to the ceremony. As I began to understand the implications of dying in the temple, my thoughts shifted away from a reluctant acceptance of death. Phoenyx would need to deal with the body, Norberto would need to deal with the public relations, and my mom would probably mistakenly think I died of a drug overdose. Although my spirit would certainly feel Grateful for the effort that Phoenyx would exert to deal with my Dead body, it was a burden that I didn't want her to carry. Even if I was at peace with passing away that day, I was concerned that people might view my death as an accident and it could give the medicine a bad name. Besides, I love my life, and not only do I love my life, but my work in this physical world is not finished. This book is not finished, I have something to say, and I think people can greatly benefit from it. No, this can't be, I can't die today! That probably sounds egocentric, but the beauty is that my opposition came from my love for life and concern for others rather than my fear of death. The funny thing is that I am *very* aware people often become convinced they are dying during psychedelic experiences. In fact, I had already written an entire chapter about it called "Death and Insanity." Regardless, this was somehow different from those rookies who mistakenly believe they are dying, this was real!

The night before we listened to a podcast with Terence McKenna and he described how most people accept and are affected by fate, but an alchemist has the ability to use their will to defy fate. That day I knew it would be necessary to use my will power to defy fate so I could complete this book and save my loved ones from cleaning up a mess. I borrowed from the movie *Doctor Strange* and imagined myself reprogramming the source code of reality to continue living. I focused on my breathing, talked to Phoenyx, purged, anything to maintain consciousness and resist the inevitable. At one point I stumbled outside and eventually crumbled to the ground and laid in the grass. Back to the soil my body goes in the never ending cycle of life I thought when suddenly I felt a hand across my back and then another. I looked over my shoulder to see Linda the wolf dog staring at me with her paws on my body as if to comfort me while I took my last breaths. Perhaps Linda was my *Holy Guardian Angel* that the tarot Hierophant card repeatedly referred to. She sure seemed like one in that moment. Later on Phoenyx came outside to check on me and we both had a good laugh about the sight of me sprawled across the temple lawn. Well, at least I could laugh during my final moments. Then the air temperature dropped and I got annoyed with itchy grass and crawling ants, so I dragged my dying body back inside.

If you are reading this book then I obviously survived that day and successfully reprogrammed the source code of reality to defy my fate. Now let's take a look at what science says. Modern research shows that regions of the brain known as the Default Mode Network (DMN) are less active during a psychedelic experience. The DMN is related to our sense of ego and identity, so when that is deactivated during ceremony the result can be a feeling of dying, also known as ego death, or more accurately temporary ego death since it returns when the experience is over. Of course we would never feel like we were dying if we didn't identify with our egos to begin with. What is really happening is the white, male, American, non-religious, only child, university educated, author, who likes backpacking, dislikes barking dogs and owns an iPhone is dying. But what remains, a dead body? Probably not, though I didn't quite find out. What I do know is that on lower doses the ego diminishes more slowly and less dramatically, and what remains is quite beautiful, something that I would call the Higher Self. That near death experience reminded me how incredibly clever the mind can be. Eckhart Tolle explains how the mind is concerned with survival and will do anything to maintain a dominant role in our lives. When I began to lose my fear of death, the mind quickly adjusted and tempted me with my love for life. Brilliant!

When he returned from his travels Norberto assured me that nobody physically dies during an Ayahuasca ceremony. Of course a person having severe preexisting physical conditions or taking contraindicated pharmaceuticals could, but definitely not a healthy person. According to his mentor Baixinha, Ayahuasca does a great job of preparing us for death by helping us face our fear of this next step into the unknown. Ideally this training will allow us to more gracefully transition out of our bodies by giving us a preview of what's to come. He also explained that for the death of the ego to be a complete process the ego needs to truly believe it is happening, otherwise the benefits are not fully received, and those benefits are quite profound. A person can be permanently changed when the ego dies, he said. For this reason when a participant is panicking during ceremony and asking for help he will typically agree with them, "Yes, you are dying." Not the comforting words you would hope to hear, but technically this is true, and to say otherwise could prevent an amazing transformation from occurring. Unfortunately I missed my opportunity, but I suspect it won't be the last.

When Psychedelics have been receiving attention lately in scientific research that demonstrates their ability to help terminal cancer patients accept their condition. I wonder why I seem to have the opposite reaction, avoidance. Perhaps because a terminal patient truly is on the verge of dying, while I am in good health and have no reason to suspect the end is near, so it comes as more of a surprise. Regardless, I'm curious about where Juremuasca would have taken me had I not fought so fiercely? Some people skydive from airplanes or bungee jump off bridges, but I prefer a more gradual approach. I don't think one is better than the other. Taking small steps is my usual style and after that day I moved a little bit closer to overcoming my greatest fear.

"There is a road, no simple highway
Between the dawn and dark of night
And if you go, noone may follow
That path is for, your steps alone"

-Ripple, by Grateful Dead

Together we Ascend

We both had the pleasure of attending one of Norberto's three-day workshops in the past and have benefitted immensely from it. Phoenyx has actually participated in many more than me, including the four-day version. However, neither of us ever attended the ten-day retreat on his property, and as a result had not yet experienced an Ayahuasca hike. A what? The concept is difficult to imagine due to the reputation Ayahuasca has of being a night medicine, and since most people hike when the sun is up, the two words are usually not found together. We can probably thank the indigenous Shipibo of the Peruvian Amazon for that impression since their tribe is most famously associated with Ayahuasca, and they typically hold ceremony after dark. While Norberto has great respect for the medicine, he is not exactly a traditional kind of guy. As I said earlier, the unconventional style of this neo-shaman comes from his background with the Santo Daime church, the Indian mystic Osho and other disciplines. He is not indigenous and does not practice as a tribal shaman would. The Santo Daime church often holds ceremony during daytime, and at night the lights are likely to be turned on. Consequently, my first time at one of his workshops was also my first time drinking Ayahuasca at midday.

I was very curious to combine two of my favorite activities, hiking and holding ceremony. Besides, after only leaving the property for a single time in the past five weeks to visit the nearby town, we felt ready to explore. Before Norberto and his partner had left to go traveling I asked him for directions. Following the hills above the temple, the cattle pasture switches to rainforest. He had pointed to the location where the trail that he takes retreat participants on begins, and gave further instructions for completing the trip. After two or three hours of hiking there is a geographic formation that is a well-known destination for residents in the area. At the top of a mountain there is a large rock balancing atop another rock bigger than a house, which is also sitting upon a massive rock that is as big as an ocean ship. Norberto had mentioned that on a clear day the view from up there is magnificent, and it would be a great place to stop for lunch before heading back to the property, or perhaps to have a second shot of medicine. He also said the dogs would love to come along for our adventure.

The secret to hiking on Ayahuasca is not to drink so much that your outer journey becomes an inner journey as you lay on the ground purging and unable to continue. This of course happens at times, but we wanted to ascend that mountain so we would consume what Sasha Shulgin refers to as a *Museum Level*, "A slightly-over-threshold level which allows public activities to be entered into without attracting attention." After all, the geological art we intended to see that day was a popular local destination, so there was a real possibility of encountering other hikers. This was a situation we never had to worry about under the protection of the temple on Norberto's isolated property. We began our ceremony as usual and drank a small shot of Juremuasca, then marched up the hill through the pasture. We had been waiting for a day with clear skies, to appreciate the distant views from the peak, and as a result the blazing sun seemed like it would melt me before we even reached the shade. Covered in sweat, I began to feel the medicine coming on as we entered the forest. The beginning section is so steep that you need to grab onto trees just to pull yourself up the hill. I probably would have been going through a process, if it wasn't for the fact that I needed to focus on the task at hand. I was on a mission to climb that hill, and anytime I stopped to catch my breath the mosquitos reminded me to keep moving.

After what seemed like eternity we eventually reached the main trail and the grade decreased a few degrees. Along the way Lukey kept stopping for rest. Even in the shade it was hot hiking uphill. The Juremuasca must have been working because I began feeling compassion for that stubborn dog who would often annoy me with his obsessive barking every time the cows came too close to the fence. To be fair, it probably kept the cows from breaking through more times than they otherwise would have if he was more relaxed. I sometimes wondered how many beautiful exotic birds we were missing back on the property because the barking dogs scared them away. I would occasionally see a glimpse of a toucan near the cabin, or a flock of green parrots flying overhead, but none ever came close enough to see clearly. In this case the idea of the dogs charging ahead of us didn't bother me too much because their presence would probably scare away any snakes that might be in the vicinity. Lukey continued to stop for rest as he rapidly panted. Was he overheating? There is no water on the ridgeline, and I don't know if they drank enough in the morning. Suddenly Lukey burst into the forest chasing who knows what, probably a colorful bird that I would have liked to see. My compassion disappeared, as I yelled to the alpha dog, "You're not leading the pack; if you're too hot then stop wasting your energy chasing birds!"

When we finally reached the reward at the end of our journey there was a rope that we used to pull ourselves up a short, but steep section. The wolf pack looked like mountain goats as they somehow managed to follow us up the inclined wall. Because of the oppressive heat and mosquitos that tormented us, I couldn't imagine being able to actually enjoy the destination, but a cool breeze atop the exposed rock formation instantly blew all our troubles away. The view from the top was amazing, and in 360 degrees all around us we could see the same pattern, cattle pastures carved from the Atlantic Rainforest that blanketed the large hills. It pains me to think about the world's forests being destroyed, but at least it wasn't a complete clearcut, and some habitat still remains. There were no other hikers to deal with, but it didn't matter because we were feeling the tiredness more than the DMT at that point, and had probably already sweat most of it out while coming up. Lunch for the day was sweet pancioca wraps filled with wild banana, coconut oil, local honey and a pinch of cinnamon. We also prepared a savory version with egg, avocado, coconut oil, mustard and salt. Panciocas, pancakes made from tapioca flour, were my latest and greatest kitchen creation. Tapioca is extracted from cassava, also known as yuca or manioc. I was super happy to discover this Brazilian staple because cassava is a root, which is the part of a plant that does *not* trigger my food allergies. Almost all other wraps, and the flour used to make them, contain grains, which means that I haven't enjoyed the pleasure of eating a delicious wrap in years. Not only is tapioca compatible with my diet, but it has a cohesive property that makes it stronger than wheat; the perfect ingredient for a durable wrap. I suppose the only downside is that they are not certified organic, so who knows how they were grown? They are also nearly pure carbohydrates, so best to eat in moderation, and balance them with some toppings high in fat and protein. Maybe someday I will get to the root cause of these food allergies, but until then root wraps provide a nice alternative.

After lunch we decided to do some Rapé before heading back down. Rapé (in Portuguese, *r* is pronounced like *h*, so it's *ha-pay*) is a non-psychedelic blend of tobacco and plants in the form of an extremely fine dust, mixed with the ash of tree bark. It is produced for medicinal purposes by tribes in the Amazon who keep their recipes, ratios and ingredients secret. Rapé is consumed by blowing air from your mouth through a V-shaped applicator called a kuripe, which then pushes the powder back into your nostril. There is also another applicator called a tepi, which requires a second person to blow the powder directly into your nose. With higher quantities the process is quite painful and can result in dizziness, nausea or even trigger purging, but with lower quantities I find the effect to be meditational. Rapé is a great tool for clearing the mind and taking a break in nature after sitting in front of a computer for too long. Just walk to the park, sit in the grass, take off your shoes, and... poof, a healthy little interruption. Once per day, or a few times per week is plenty for me. Of course anything in life can be abused, and there are people who pull out their kuripe too often. Even though Rapé contains tobacco it's not meant to be a regular habit like smoking cigarettes. In fact, the tribes have a much different view of tobacco than we do. They harvest the much more potent *Nicotiana rustica* rather than the *tabacum* species that is commercially sold. For them tobacco, or Mapacho as they sometimes call it, is a sacred plant, a teacher plant, a master plant that cleanses. For example, the Shipibo natives typically use Mapacho cigarettes to clear negative energies during ceremony. Standing on top of the rainforest, with freshly cleared heads, we took advantage of the privacy and elevation to honor the Norse gods with a loud rendition of the opening line to Led Zeppelin's *Immigrant Song.* "Ah-aaaaaaaaah-ah, ah-aaaaaaaaah-ah, we come from the land of the ice and snow…" I think Odin must have heard us.

My concerns for Lukey were relieved when I saw the dogs tearing apart a few plants to access the rainwater captured near the base. The bowl-shaped leaves were holding a pool of water that I didn't see, but perhaps they could smell it? This wolf pack knows some serious survival skills! Funny to think only moments earlier I was worried while watching them chase lizards near the edge of the cliff. With everyone fed, watered, and Rapéd, it was time to return to the property before sunset. I asked Phoenyx if we should take another shot of Juremuasca for the walk down, but she suggested we wait until we were closer. I was skeptical and replied, "Are you sure?" She was, so I reluctantly trusted her advice and we marched back down the hill. When we eventually reached the clearing of Norberto's pasture I sat down and pulled the medicine out of the backpack. Time for one small shot before we close ceremony and prepare dinner. In the twenty minutes it took to reach the cabin I began to feel ill. I went inside, took off my shoes and collapsed on the floor, exhausted from the long day on the trail. Minutes later I sprang to my feet and lunged toward the toilet faster than a lightning bolt. I unleashed a purge accompanied by a Viking battle roar that would have made *Thor* proud. I can only imagine how the wolf pack was reacting outside since they certainly heard me. Linda, my "Guardian Angel," probably wanted to protect me from whatever horrible beast she thought was attacking me. Nothing makes me purge like Jurema, not Ayahuasca, Huachuma or Peyote. "I guess you were right about saving the second shot until we were closer to the property," I said. No matter how wild and crazy things got in spirit land, one thing was for sure, I could always count on Phoenyx to make smart decisions. With no mountains to climb and a fresh shot of Juremuasca in our bellies we were now able to lie on the beds and actually notice the effects of an altered consciousness. Well, I *had* a fresh shot in my stomach, before bolting to the bathroom, but it must have already entered my bloodstream.

The next day we felt like *Fierce Invalids Home From Hot Climates*, a Tom Robbins novel featuring Ayahuasca in the rainforest. We were sore from the hike and needed to get some rest. Phoenyx had been reading one of his other books, *Half Asleep in Frog Pajamas*, and remarked on the synchronicity of how Robbins spoke of amphibians nearly as often as we saw and heard them. He also frequently mentioned Sirius, the bright flashing star that demanded our attention every night; the tarot; and psychedelics. Many times I've thought that our strange adventures could easily be the plot of a Robbins novel. Occasionally throughout the winter Phoenyx would jokingly ask, "Which actor will play you when Hollywood makes a movie of the book?" That's a tough question. We both agreed that *The Martian* was a great movie, it dealt with a very serious situation, being stranded on an alien planet, yet was equally light hearted as Matt Damon's character persevered to survive. Sometimes we too felt like explorers of another planet, both in this dimension and the next, so maybe Damon could do the job. Or perhaps Rami Malek would be a better match. He's the star of the *Mr. Robot* series about a brilliant hacker who wishes to "save the world" from corporate greed by attacking the computer network of a powerful bank. I don't know much about coding, but I definitely relate to his idealistic intentions. Does it sound arrogant to speak of being the star of your own movie? I'm not talking about a quest for fame and fortune. I don't need to wear expensive watches and own a giant mansion. There's already way too much of that these days. I'm talking about living a life worthy of watching, even if nobody is paying attention. To be on the screen instead of sitting in front of it. To look back over the years during your final days and have no regrets.

"Did you have a good world when you died
Enough to base a movie on?"

-The Movie, by Jim Morrison

☿

Medicinal Manure

Nearly seven weeks after arriving on the property it was time to say goodbye. The primary reason for leaving was that Norberto and his partner had returned home and our care taking services were no longer needed. The timing was right and after nine Ayahuasca and Juremuasca ceremonies we were ready for a break. Our idea was to get some rest from the extremes of living in the rainforest where our most repeated phrase seemed to be, "It's always something," as in, if it's not this problem then it's another. As beautiful as the land is it could also be quite challenging at times. While the mosquitoes were never extreme they were persistent and the only break from them was by shutting the windows at sunset. Temperatures and humidity during daytime were often too high to keep the windows closed or wear long layers, so the choice was either to be super hot or get bitten. Insect repellant wasn't an option since we were health conscious and not interested in spraying poison on our skin. Citronella oil was somewhat effective, though we didn't discover that until later. In addition, the filter on the water supply system would regularly need cleaning or sometimes get washed away during a big storm. Fixing the water system meant hiking uphill into the rainforest, which may sound nice, but when the water flow stopped daily it was frustrating and took time and energy away from doing our chores. There were also random occurrences that were inevitable when living on such a raw and rugged property bordering a vibrant rainforest. For example, one time a swarm of honeybees decided to make their home under our roof and dozens were flying around inside the cabin. Luckily honeybees are not aggressive, but we had to deter them from permanently staying by smoking them out. Another time the cattle broke the barbed wire fence and escaped from the pasture to our living area. Fortunately Norberto had trained us for such a scenario and we successfully herded them back through and mended the fence. The wind could be very powerful and during a particularly strong storm part of the roof was damaged on one of the cabins, which required some minor repair work. I complained when these events occurred, but looking back, it was all totally worth it. A small price to pay in exchange for the experience of a lifetime, food, lodging, medicine and enough material to write an entire book.

Reactions vary from people who arrive on the land for their first time to attend a workshop. According to Norberto some immediately worry upon arriving after realizing how isolated and disconnected from civilization they are. Others have been enchanted when they first arrive, but eventually feel overwhelmed by the energy of the land and need to work through the situation. There is plenty of time to sit around and simply stare at the green forest, which can trigger people who would normally be distracted from their problems by electronic devices. A few paying participants have even left the retreats early because they simply can't handle the isolation and the resulting emotions that arise. On the opposite end of the spectrum are those who declare the land to be a paradise. I fell into the latter category, though it is important to understand the difference between being a caretaker and a paying participant. As the caretaker there is nobody to carry your food and luggage up the long steep hill for you. There is no cook to prepare all the meals, especially the meal following an exhausting ceremony. When no water comes out of the faucet, guess who needs to fix the problem? Paradise? Absolutely, but with a price to pay.

Norberto never had high demands of us other than to feed the animals, watch the property and do whatever small projects we felt like doing. However, the challenges of living on this wild land were multiplied by the challenges of drinking the medicine. Coming to an isolated rainforest property and drinking nearly a liter of Ayahuasca and Jurema for the first time without a shaman present required some adjustments. Fortunately though, Phoenyx and I complemented each other. My years of wilderness backpacking prepared me for the nature side of the experience, while the year Phoenyx spent assisting Norberto prepared her for the emotional and psychological side.

The previous summer I had earned a certificate as a coach specializing in helping people prepare for, navigate through and integrate after Sacred Medicine experiences. Integration is an important topic that until recently was largely being ignored by the Sacred Medicine community. I believe it helps to distinguish between two types of integration: the days immediately after a ceremony versus the weeks and months after. For my certificate program we focused mostly on the weeks and months after when it is important to transform temporary states into permanent traits. In other words, applying the insights gained during ceremony to your daily routine. The plants can't do everything for us, we still need to take responsibility and make an effort to change our lives.

In Brazil we focused more on short-term integration. We did our best to space the ceremonies by always reserving three to five days between drinking the medicine for resting. In comparison, at most weekend workshops participants drink for three consecutive days, and it is not uncommon to drink up to nine out of ten days at a longer retreat, including those offered by Norberto. I obviously admire our shaman, but I sometimes question this pace. If it's accelerated transformation you want then drinking so much in so little time is one way to do it. That is assuming you properly integrate the experience afterwards, a service that many facilitators don't offer, and something that participants rarely seem to prioritize. Norberto doesn't currently offer any integration services besides the next-morning sharing circles that are standard for most retreats. However, nobody is forced to go home immediately afterwards, and the option exists to pay a modest food fee that covers the cost of staying longer for those who want. He also provides a list of professional counselors who are familiar with the medicine for participants that need support following a workshop. The reality is the average person simply doesn't have the luxury of drinking nine times spaced over seven weeks. We were blessed to have the opportunity to drink at the pace that was ideal for our needs.

When we weren't busy swatting mosquitoes, fixing water supply filters, herding cattle, chasing bees or mending roofs, the rainforest offered a perfect place to rest. I know that may have sounded sarcastic, but the setting seriously couldn't be topped. There was complete silence in terms of human made mechanical noise. At most there might be the faint hum of an airplane flying high above once per day. Other than that it was the soothing sounds of birds chirping, rain falling, frogs croaking, wind blowing, insects buzzing, rooster crowing and the occasional cow mooing. Besides the Portuguese-speaking neighbor who sometimes stopped by to work on a project there were no humans to interact with in our altered states. It is very common to feel exhausted (we call it "smashed potatoes" after once reading a funny translation on a Peruvian menu) in the days following a ceremony, and this is nothing to worry about, but not how you want to feel while trying to have an intelligent conversation with another person.

In addition to the silence and privacy, another huge advantage of resting on the land was the minimal access to electronics. Yes, there was solar powered satellite Internet available, but we made an effort to avoid it. In fact, we discovered that going online for only thirty minutes the day after ceremony left us feeling ill. These days it is nearly impossible to have an electronic fast unless you either have extreme discipline or attend something like a Vipassana meditation retreat that prohibits mobile devices. I enjoy the many benefits of information, entertainment and social media that Wi-Fi brings to me, but the last thing I want to do is interrupt my transformational process with a news headline about another stupid comment made by a politician.

One thing I found very effective for the integration process was to do small chores around the property. Norberto left many young Chacrunas that needed to be planted, and since they grow best in shade he also left some young guava trees. While my physical stamina was temporarily diminished by the large quantities of medicine we were drinking, I found it quite satisfying to go out for a couple hours and plant a few Chacrunas until I began feeling too hot, itchy or tired. Another such project that occupied my time was the collection of cow manure. We collected the manure to store in a large tank where small worms were living. As the worms consumed the manure, the resulting product was fertile compost that gave the young Chacrunas a big nutritional advantage over the wild plants surrounding them.

Some may wince at the idea of collecting poop and feeding it to worms, but the process was actually quite satisfying and maybe even a bit poetic. The elimination and decomposition of that which no longer serves us to feed the growth of something better. This natural cycle was a direct parallel to the Ayahuasca experience. My role as a worm farmer connected me to nature, a connection that is extremely deficient in these modern days of huge, noisy, crowded, polluted, steel and concrete cities. Yes, mother Ayahuasca not only heals by helping us process emotional traumas from our childhood, but she can also heal by reconnecting us to the natural world. Ultimately, connection is the name of the game, connection to each other, to nature, and most importantly, to our Higher Selves.

Although awareness of integration seems to be increasing I still see people drinking loads of Ayahuasca and then rush, rush, rush the next morning to fly back home. To be honest I consider that to be a big mistake. People spend so much time, energy and money to attend workshops, endure all of the emotional stress, suffer from nausea and physical discomfort, and then travel through a busy airport the next day in a sensitive and vulnerable state. Norberto says we remain open for about three days after ceremony and should be very cautious of what we are exposed to during that time. I can attest to that, during my first workshop with him it took days for me to return back to Earth. I can't imagine squeezing into a crowded airplane with all those strangers and whatever problems they are dealing with in that condition. Two steps forward and one step back is normal for most people following a workshop, but rushing like this sounds to me like two steps forward and one and a half steps back. It's still progress, but much less than it could be. Perhaps it would help the business people who always hurry back to work if I spoke more in the language of efficiency, as in you make an investment in your health and earn a much larger profit when the proper amount of time is scheduled afterwards for rest and integration. If you reserve one week for attending a workshop then the default should be to reserve at least an additional week after for eating good food, sleeping, walking in nature, taking naps and reflecting on the prior week.

Having said all that, we definitely reserved three days for rest before our flight to Peru where we planned to take a break and transform our temporary states to permanent traits in the Andes Mountains.

Intermission

Huachuma in Peru

The time had come for a change of scenery, so we boarded a flight and headed to the Valle Sagrado in the Andes Mountains of Peru where we first met three years ago. Since we had only made a single trip from the property in Brazil to the nearest town, a two-hour walk plus a fifteen minute bus ride, we were completely isolated except for a couple visits from the neighbor who didn't speak English, so traveling through airports was a slight shock to the system. From seven hundred meters up to three thousand, the climate instantly switched from hot and humid to cool and dry, at least when the seasonal rain wasn't falling. The small town we were visiting not only offered a change of scenery and climate, but it is also known for being one of the Sacred Medicine capitals of the world. If you want to know the name of this town, you at least need to do a little work; I can't just give you the keys to Kamar-Taj for free…

There is one plant in particular that people come here to experience, the mescaline containing San Pedro cactus locally known as Huachuma. While many people travel to the Amazon Rainforest to drink Ayahuasca in its native habitat, some travelers also visit the higher elevations of the Andes to drink Huachuma in its natural environment. However, for most people at this point in time Huachuma still remains hidden in the shadows of Ayahuasca. Fortunately, the plant is easily available for those who know where to look. Unlike most other places in the world, the Peruvian government honors the ancient traditions of its people by classifying the cactus as legal, as it should be, and as it has been for millennia.

Earlier I mentioned that the timing was right to leave Brazil and take a break from Juremuasca, so why fly across the continent in pursuit of another sacrament? Besides the fact that I enjoy the experience and greatly benefit from it, Huachuma is believed by many in the plant medicine community to improve the integration process when consumed following Ayahuasca. To better understand the word *integrate* it helps to consider the opposite word, disintegrate. Think of Ayahuasca as the deconstructionist, dynamite or wrecking ball that knocks down the obstacles in our mind that prevent us from healing and progressing. If you wait long enough following an Ayahuasca workshop the mind will certainly be rebuilt as a better version than it previously was, especially if you properly use the tools of integration. However, if Ayahuasca is the bulldozer then Huachuma must be the architect, hammer or crane that builds a new and improved mind. You could rebuild without assistance, but considering that Huachuma is often referred to as the Grandfather, why not accept the help of a wise old man?

Grandfather is a powerful yet gentle medicine that allows the person more freedom to guide the experience in a direction of their choice, unlike Ayahuasca, which can take you to a place whether you want to go there or not. Imagine the environment both plants come from, Ayahuasca in the dark crowded rainforest offers few options other than forward through the narrow path. Huachuma on the other hand grows in a wide-open mountain range that allows you to choose your destination. For that reason I find it easier to be copilot of the spaceship with Huachuma than with Ayahuasca. It is profound yet playful, introspective yet talkative, and you can enjoy the beauty of an expanded consciousness without relentlessly being presented with traumas, fears, and other difficult mental and emotional issues that need work. That being said, this peaceful medicine certainly does come with a challenge and is not always an easy walk through the park. I believe some people struggle with that freedom, as if they don't know where to go with the infinite number of doors that can open. North, south, east, west, up, down, in, out, past, future, this dimension or the next. Also, since Huachuma is longer lasting (at least twelve hours) it can be exhausting on a high dose when all those doors open and loads of information come streaming through hour after hour.

During our six weeks in Peru I had the fortune to drink Huachuma on four separate occasions. The first time was under the guidance of a local man with a solid reputation around town. He provided ceremonies in a beautiful garden with a great view of the surrounding valley. It was the first time we actually drank medicine with another human after spending seven weeks in Brazil. The irony being that following our initiation of drinking Ayahuasca alone, we were now paying a facilitator to drink Huachuma, which I find to be a much more forgiving plant medicine. The gentle nature of Huachuma makes it easier for a person to experience it without a facilitator, though I wouldn't recommend it for your first time. A mature person who has looked within and is very aware of their mental and emotional situation should be able to at least drink a small dose alone if they wish. Although I've drunk alone many times before, in this case I was willing to pay the fee and enjoy the presence of the other participants. Plus, the facilitator always offers words of wisdom that I appreciate, including a demonstration the day before of how to prepare the brew from a fresh column of cactus. The most valuable lesson he taught me that day was how to be with others who are struggling with the experience. Huachuma is known to be a heart opening medicine and the resulting compassion that arises can tempt you to assist those in need. Unlike Ayahuasca, I find it surprisingly easy to hold a conversation under the influence of a strong dose of Huachuma. However, talking to your neighbor can stimulate the rational mind and be a distraction from listening to the inner whisper spoken by the plant. The cactus is a much more qualified coach than I would ever be, but initially people don't always appreciate this. Instead they seek the connection from a neighbor who might make them feel better amid their confusion and loneliness. I wanted to help a fellow participant, but I learned that in the long run, silence was the best way to support him.

For the second ceremony I decided to drink alone to save money and avoid paying a facilitator. That morning I prepared some Huachuma powder that Phoenyx had purchased from a big market in the city of Cusco. While the consensus seems to be that cooking fresh cactus is definitely the ideal way of making medicine, using dried powder is often much easier. The process is relatively simple and involves simmering the powder in water for at least an hour or two at a very low temperature and stirring often to avoid burning the bottom of the pot.

With the brew in my backpack I hiked up to the archeological park fifteen hundred meters above town and sat down to partake at the Temple of the Sun. Having witnessed a rainbow in Brazil during the Full Moon New Year celebration, I was delighted to see another one at the site of an ancient temple. This time I was so high in elevation that I actually looked down upon the rainbow in the valley below. It felt as if the blessings were showering upon me that winter, and the gods were pleased with my ways. On the hike down I stopped for an amazing panorama view of the valley and expressed gratitude out loud to the Apus, the spirits of the surrounding mountains who are believed to protect inhabitants of the region.

For the third ceremony we began the day from our hotel room. A look through the window to the courtyard revealed a healthy cactus growing higher than the second story rooms. I doubt the owners have ever harvested a piece of this giant because it is no longer the custom of the local Quechua people. While it is quite common to see them plant San Pedro as landscaping, you are more likely to see a traveling gringo like me drinking it than them. Perhaps the plant was more widely consumed prior to the Spanish conquest, but these days the natives are mostly Catholics who unfortunately would rather drink a consciousness contracting, corn-based alcohol than a consciousness expanding, cactus-based medicine. Despite our differences I can't think of a single time that I had a real problem with any of the Quechua. They drink more and party louder than I prefer, but are always extremely polite and peaceful people.

After leaving the room we walked over to the stunning botanical garden and spent a few hours enjoying the scenery and petting the white garden cat. Yes, walking through a small town and interacting with people is very much possible on Huachuma, especially in a medicine friendly place like Kamar-Taj. There were many San Pedro on display and when I asked the gardener if he considers the cactus a medicine, he replied that it was, but not for him. It was a surprising answer from a man who has been maintaining that garden and growing San Pedro there for forty years. I know that everyone has different tastes, but it made me think the Spanish did a great job of destroying the natives' connection to spirit.

The Spanish may have crushed the connection, but they certainly did not eradicate the plant. Back at the hotel I noticed a small cactus arm sitting in the courtyard that the owners had discarded after pruning their giant plant. The arm had been abandoned for weeks and was beginning to deteriorate. It clearly would not be appreciated, so we took it to the kitchen and applied our newly learned cooking skills for preparing fresh medicine. We coordinated our fourth ceremony to occur not only on the full moon, but also the three year anniversary since we first met, which happened to be at a Huachuma full moon party here in Kamar-Taj. Unfortunately, this time our favorite Huachumero would not be hosting any parties due to his busy schedule. Since we were well accustomed to drinking alone, it would not be a problem. On full moon day we hiked up a path bordering a small stream that led to the agricultural terraces at the base of the archeological park just outside of town. Our first time cooking fresh cactus was a success as that little cactus arm came on surprisingly strong. Later on that night we celebrated our accomplishment with a visit to our favorite Huachumero's restaurant back in town.

When people see him for the first time I suspect that many make the mistake of dismissing him as *the waiter*, or perhaps just another traveler because he doesn't look Quechua, not realizing that he knows more about Huachuma than perhaps anybody in the valley. Some have been outraged by the thought of him throwing full moon Huachuma *parties*, complete with DJs pumping out loud music until sunrise. One of the first lessons taught by Sacred Medicines is not to be fooled by the illusions of the world. Upon further examination one realizes that our favorite Huachumero may be extremely unconventional, but he still has much respect for the medicine, provides utmost care for every participant, and has perhaps more to offer than a stereotypical feather-wearing, flute-playing, tobacco-blowing shaman. He is both kind and cool, traditional and modern, but above all he has a big heart. In many ways he reminds me of Norberto, a down to earth facilitator who doesn't take himself too seriously. He doesn't have a long waiting list or serve medicine to Hollywood celebrities, and hopefully it stays that way. The parties are attended by invitation only and guests are carefully screened for compatibility with the medicine and the other participants.

That night we wandered into his restaurant very much appreciating the effects of the abandoned cactus we rescued from the hotel, yet still suffering a bit from a persistent case of Giardia, a digestive parasite. When our favorite Huachumero approached our table to take orders, I casually inquired, what dish would you recommend for someone coming off a strong dose of Huachuma AND dealing with Giardia??? He instantly replied without missing a beat and suggested a couple different soups, with slight modifications for our unique mental and digestive state. HA, where else on planet Earth can you ask the waiter a question like that and receive such a helpful suggestion? The only thing he failed to do was offer us a Tinidazole, a mild pharmaceutical, for desert. Normally I am an all-natural, plant-based kind of guy who avoids synthetic chemicals as much as possible. In this case, after a week of consuming powerful herbal remedies without success, it was time to remove those disruptive microorganisms with the assistance of modern technology. There was an upcoming long-distance flight, and we were growing weaker each day due to not being able to properly digest food, so I reluctantly swallowed the pills. Tinidazole cured Giardia rapidly and had no noticeable side effects.

Prior to leaving Brazil I had told Norberto that we would be on the other side of the continent and to message me if he needed any more help. A few weeks after arriving in Peru he requested that we return to watch the property a second time while he was away traveling. I had hoped to be invited back but was not expecting anything as he had mentioned the possibility of hiring a permanent caretaker after we left. A big smile spread across my face as I read his email, though I suspected that Phoenyx would not be thrilled at the thought of returning to the heat and mosquitoes so soon. I shared the exciting news and gave her some time to think about it. A couple days later she summoned her warrior spirit and was ready for more.

After receiving our invitation for the next destination we did our best to rest and enjoy the comforts of civilization before it was time to go back. Ultimately we would have six total weeks of long term Ayahuasca integration before returning to do it all over again. Kamar-Taj has many nice restaurants where you can eat a variety of delicious foods that are not found in other places of the world, like alpaca burgers or Coca cookies. It was a nice break not always needing to cook food and wash the dishes. After weeks of isolation there was an opportunity to connect with fascinating people who are also walking the Medicine Path. To simply sit in a café and listen to conversations around me was a form of entertainment. Within three minutes you are almost guaranteed to hear some of the following words: Ayahuasca, Huachuma, ceremony, medicine, spirit, chakra, energy, hermano or hermana. Within ten minutes you would probably hear them all. A walk through the streets reveals shamanic shops catering to gringos that sell everything imaginable, including: Coca leaves, Sananga eye drops, Rapé snuff, kuripe applicators, Mapacho cigarettes, Peruvian crystals, alpaca vests, Andean flutes, Kambo sticks, and jewelry. There are posters on windows advertising Amazon plant dietas, Cacao Kirtan sessions, yoga classes, sound healing performances, various forms of massage, astrological readings, and of course ceremonies, ceremonies, ceremonies. I appreciate the balance that still exists between local Quechua people maintaining their traditional ways of living, and having traveler friendly options available. Let's hope the town continues to be unique and avoids becoming a crowded spiritual Disneyland.

Beyond these wonderful treats the little town quickly irritated me. Despite the small population it soon felt like living in New York City. Screaming kids, barking dogs, beeping cars and the high energy of the valley were testing me following weeks of isolation in the rainforest. There were frequent celebrations that occurred any day of the week and sometimes lasted until two in the morning, complete with fireworks and loud speakers. It reminds me of the movie *The Accountant* starring Ben Affleck as an autistic accountant, who also happens to be an assassin. There is a scene where the father considers enrolling his son at a center for people with autism. The director assures the father that his place is the best option for his son because it's a sensory friendly environment. The father defiantly replies, "If loud noises and bright lights bother him, he needs more of it, not less. The world is *not* a sensory friendly place, and that's where he needs to learn to live." This is not a strategy that I endorse. Huachuma and other Sacred Medicines can increase our sensitivity and make us aware of the things in our life that cause harm. Once we become aware of the destructive forces around us, then how do we learn to coexist in a threatening world? I guess the easiest answer is to avoid or change what you can, and try not to dwell on what you can't. In my case I was determined to rent a quiet apartment far outside of town during our next visit, and until then, wear earplugs at night and throw corncobs at the dogs barking outside my window.

Immediately upon returning to Brazil it became apparent that something had shifted. The sun was still hot and the mosquitoes still buzzed, but Phoenyx had a newfound appreciation for the land. She was more relaxed than before. To make life easier, the season was shifting from summer to fall in the Southern Hemisphere, and Norberto had fixed the water supply filter to clog less often. As for me, I was happy to escape from civilization and eager to return to my wilderness playground. This former cat lover missed his wolf pack. The odd thing is that integration of Ayahuasca *did* occur, and even though I didn't notice it while we were in Peru, Huachuma seemed to have built us back up nonetheless. Madre and Grandfather, a potent combination indeed.

Brazil, Part Two

Umbanda

I love the freedom that a Norberto workshop provides. It begins with a simple yet powerful opening prayer followed by some singing while the medicine is poured. He then assigns the group an exercise to do after we drink, rather than lying on our mattresses and anxiously waiting for the DMT to enter our system. Since Norberto has a reputation for serving strong medicine it would be too difficult to coordinate these kinds of exercises during the peak of the experience, and people would probably be too exhausted to do them at the end. He takes full advantage of the transition phase from sober to altered when we are very impressionable yet still functional.

For example, during my first workshop we were directed to eye gaze for a few minutes while holding hands with a person we never met before. As a person who sometimes avoided eye contact I can honestly say my social skills improved in the months that followed. One of my favorite exercises was doing the Osho Kundalini Meditation, which involved vigorous shaking of the body and then some flowing, dance like movements, followed by sitting and then laying still. I'm quite certain it worked because soon after my upper body was buzzing with energy in a way that it never has before, and I saw beautiful geometric shapes and colors. I remember that afternoon as being an especially enjoyable experience that I described as heaven on Earth. I wondered if this was similar to Satori, the Zen Buddhist term for a temporary glimpse of enlightenment.

One exercise that was extremely effective for me was to think of my male family members while we walked around the room during an ancestral lineage release. Barely thirty minutes after drinking and I already had the urge to purge. Fortunately for the other participants I had the awareness to excuse myself from the room before the volcano erupted. As I dropped to my knees and waited for the vomit to flow I was surprised to instead release the absolute loudest yell of my entire life, later known as the *Incredible Hulk* yell. I'm normally a quiet and calm guy, but this noise must have sent small animals far away into hiding. I believe the yell was directly related to the exercise and acted as an audible alternative to the typical vomit purge most people have. The explosion was a major breakthrough for me that released anger, frustration or some kind of energy that probably would have led to disease had it remained in my system. There is no doubt that yell served a purpose and was desperately needed for me to progress through the healing process.

Once the exercises are complete the music begins as his partner sings and plays guitar. From that point on Norberto steps aside and the relationship is primarily between the participant and the medicine. He is there to hold the space, to monitor the situation and ensure everyone is safe. Support is always provided when someone is really struggling and guidance is available when requested, but he does his best not to interfere. It's an opportunity to have a therapeutic process in whatever form it takes whether that means yelling, crying, shaking or flopping around like a fish out of water. The only basic rule that must be followed is to show respect for your neighbors, the place and hopefully the medicine.

Even though a Norberto workshop has little resemblance to a religious event there is no doubt that the Santo Daime church has influenced him. How could he not have been, after learning from his mentor Baixinha for many years? Baixinha was a prominent leader of the local church and she was largely responsible for bringing the Afro-Brazilian practice of Umbanda to the Santo Daime. Umbanda is a syncretic religion that combines Spiritism, Catholicism, African traditions and indigenous beliefs. Although the two religions are related and share many things in common, I think it is important to be clear that an Umbanda ceremony does not represent a typical Santo Daime session.

Since I had such appreciation for the benefits I received from the services Norberto provided, I wanted to learn more about his background, and when the opportunity appeared to attend an Umbanda ceremony known as a Gira at the church where he came from, I knew it would be necessary to go. Out of respect for the Umbanda religion, the Santo Daime church and the members who have now expanded beyond the borders of Brazil to countries around the world, I want to make the disclaimer that I am nowhere close to understanding how they function, or exactly what their purpose is. The following are simply the observations and experiences of a first timer.

I completed a form when I arrived regarding my state of health along with other questions about my personal beliefs that would indicate whether it was appropriate or not for the church to serve me Ayahuasca, which they refer to as Daime. A translator was provided to help read the form, explain a few basic rules and answer any additional questions that I may have throughout the day. The event began in an orderly manner with the men on the right side of the room and the women on the left. Everyone wore simple white clothing with the exception of senior members who had a patch on their shirts to display rank. We stood on straight lines that were marked on the floor and were directed to fill in the gaps anytime a person left to use the toilet or take a break. A senior member was always there to guide people from the left to the right and from the back to the front.

I'm sure there were reasons for all of this, and it was probably related to building the energy of the room and maintaining the unity of the group, yet I struggled with the concept of combining Ayahuasca with so many rules. After all, many would say that psychedelics dissolve boundaries and the institutions that create them, so why organize a religion around Ayahuasca in the first place? I had grown so accustomed over the years to people sometimes rolling around on the floor, yelling and vomiting that the thought of bringing order to that chaos seemed absurd. Despite these observations I decided to continue as open minded as possible to whatever unfolded. The room and everyone in it was smudged with some kind of smoking incense. We began with some songs and hand clapping and soon after lined up to drink a small shot of watery Daime. According to my translator the intention was not to have strong Ayahuasca experiences, rather the Daime was served as a sacrament to open us up to spirit, and for many in the room that day it certainly did.

Having few expectations of what was to come I was surprised to watch the first woman step forward to receive an entity known as a Caboclo into her body, and then another woman, and then another. A Caboclo is the spirit of an indigenous person. Before long their altar in the center of the room was surrounded by senior members who appeared to be channeling these Caboclo spirits. I don't mean any disrespect, and I know this was not supposed to be a day at the circus, but it was very entertaining, in fact I was fascinated and had never seen anything like that in my entire life. The Caboclos appeared to be different but had similar characteristics like the way they distorted the medium's face with scowls or squinted eyes. Many had a certain way of standing, dancing and using hand gestures. The mediums appeared to be average middle class Brazilians, but suddenly their manners were very primitive, almost like I was watching a tribal ritual thousands of years ago. The most noticeable behavior was the way they were constantly brushing off their shoulders and heads and then flicking away the residue. I assumed the Caboclos were removing some negative energy from their hosts that must accumulate on a medium's body over time. Once all the senior members had been occupied by spirits those of us who remained were then invited to the center and paired with a medium. My Caboclo made bird-like sounds as he wiped the harmful energy from my body with some kind of fresh picked branches and leaves. He did a very thorough job and strange as it all may sound I was very grateful for the opportunity to be cleansed. There were no immediate effects, but who knows, maybe the benefits would come later? The group was now cleansed and prepared for the second half, but first we would break for lunch.

Having spent time in Iquitos, Peru and learning about the ways of the Shipibo natives from the area, I knew how important it was for them to follow a strict dieta the days before and after an Ayahuasca ceremony. The Shipibo promote the abstinence of sex, drugs, alcohol, sugar, salt, oil, spices and most meat. All that remains are some fruits, vegetables and bland fish. Because of this I was surprised to see the church serving large plates of cheesy chicken and rice. I guess it doesn't matter to them since little emphasis is placed on the small shot of watery Daime served. I must confess that during the break my conditioned modern mind had moments of skepticism. Was this real, were they actually channeling spirits or was this all some sort of act? What do you expect from a guy who was raised in a culture where spiritism is virtually extinct and psychoactive teas are illegal? Regardless, whatever we did during the first half must have been working because I felt great. The group then returned to the church for their second shot of Daime and what was to come next.

Back on the property the previous caretakers had informed us that during the ceremony there is an opportunity to directly request assistance from the spirits. Phoenyx had encouraged me to ask for help with the food allergies that have been bothering me for the past eight years. Those food allergies were part of the reason I first decided to drink Ayahuasca in Peru. Again my conditioned modern mind was having doubts about the possibility of spirits clearing food allergies that doctors and practitioners could not, but I came all the way to Brazil, so why not give it a try?

While the first half featured Caboclo spirits, the second half appeared to be the spirits of old Africans who died enslaved, known as Preto Velhos. This time when the mediums received the spirits they began to hunch over and slowly and shakily walk with the assistance of a supporter. For example, I saw a thirty-year-old man walking like he was ninety while a fifty-year-old man helped him to his bench. When it was my turn to leave the white marked line on the floor and enter the space in the center of the room I was paired with a man who I soon learned was channeling a woman known as Maria. After the medium examined my hands for a few minutes the translator told Maria my request. She asked a few questions and then instructed me to, "Go to church and bathe in the ocean seven times; pray for 'strength, protection and work.'" After this I was to perform a ritual, offering the foods that trigger me to the ocean, and then gradually reintroduce them to my diet during the following weeks. It was difficult to believe this would cure me of my allergies, but what's the worst that could happen? Perhaps I could find a Santo Daime church in the US to attend next summer? Despite serving

Ayahuasca, a controlled substance, they do exist there and are currently protected by the freedom of religion, although the legal status seems unstable and subject to challenges.

The day ended with the mediums channeling young children spirits known as Crianças, and running around the room playing games. I saw a fifty-year-old woman licking a candy sucker and acting like she was five. One thirty-year-old man was tricking an adult by taking his shoe and hiding it. They danced, jumped, sang songs, wore ribbons in their hair and were quite joyful. It was a fun and light way of ending the day yet I was cold and my feet hurt so I sat on a bench and crossed my arms to retain heat. An elder quickly approached to remind me of another church rule. As she spoke in Portuguese I politely requested, "English?" She paused, assessed the situation and then twitched her head and neck a few times before explaining to me in clear English that we do not cross our legs or arms in church because it blocks the reception of energy. It reminded me of the civilians in *The Matrix* movie who twitch while they are suddenly possessed by an agent in pursuit of Neo. Many of the Brazilians I met spoke little to no English. After all I witnessed that day my imagination was now activated, and the sharp line between possible and impossible was blurring. If these people channel spirits, what else can they do? Did this lady just download English from the spiritual realm or was she simply bilingual? I guess that I will never know, as we didn't meet again before I left.

At one point during the day I was trying to read a sign hanging above the main entrance and after struggling for a few minutes with my terrible knowledge of Portuguese the translation finally hit me, "Vida, Saúde, Felicidade, Caminhos Abertos," the prayer that Norberto uses to open and close all his ceremonies, "Life, Health, Happiness, Open Paths." Making the connection between the church sign and Norberto's workshops gave the words a greater significance and would help me to appreciate them more the next time we recited the prayer.

It was far too soon to make any judgments about what I had witnessed that day. Some would even argue that anytime is too soon to make a judgment, as it is another restriction placed on our lives by the always-classifying modern mind. It's probably best to distinguish between judging and discerning. Judging often leads to the labeling of something as good or bad, while discerning allows us to decide if something is in our best interest or not. Either way, an open mind and some time would be needed to process the experience. One thing is for certain, there was a positive energy flowing through the room that is often lacking during our private ceremonies in the temple, and that energy must be the result of all the work done to unite the community. It's no coincidence that a typical Santo Daime session is called a Work as it takes much effort to stand, dance, clap and sing hymns for long hours under the influence of a medicine that usually inspires me to lie flat on my back. I definitely appreciate the energy generated, yet wonder how they are able to do it when challenging emotions surface. After all, that's exactly how Ayahuasca heals, by bringing challenging emotions to the surface. Should people sing through an emotional process and force themselves to dance when they feel like lying on the ground and focusing within? I truly value the silence we have during our private ceremonies and wonder whether all the noise is a distraction from self-examination. Although music is traditionally used during ceremonies in many cultures, it is typically the shaman who is required to perform and not the participants. While I probably won't be joining the church and wearing a badge on my white shirt anytime soon, I definitely feel grateful for the opportunity to receive an energetic cleansing and witness the place Norberto came from.

Active Participation

It took a few days for me to process the Umbanda experience at the Santo Daime church. We were experimenting with some new batches of Ayahuasca that Norberto had left us for our second round of being caretakers on the land. To make things a little more interesting we arrived after he left the country and were not able to talk in person about the strength, type or characteristics of the medicine he left. In this case it's always best to start small and build up in dosage as needed, especially with Norberto as he has a reputation for, and I suspect takes great pride in making very potent Ayahuasca.

We started with fifty milliliters of what we believed to be Ourinho (the little golden) and to our surprise were still relatively sober a couple hours after drinking a second cup. It's not necessary to get blasted every time, but the last time we drank a hundred milliliters of Ourinho it was almost overwhelming. I believe great benefits can also come from a mild experience, and they did. Because the effects were not very noticeable, instead of laying on our mattresses in silence we eventually decided to talk. That's one of the advantages of a private ceremony, being able to speak with your neighbor without interrupting the group. Silence is usually the best way, but that day sharing insights felt more productive. Having recently returned form the church, Santo Daime was the topic of conversation in our slightly altered state, and I slowly began to realize my appreciation for their religion.

There is no middleman at that church. No priest standing in front of the room interpreting spirituality for you. Yes, there is a leader who guides the event and ensures that rules are followed in accordance with their tradition, but he/she is not the only person in the room connected to God. Everybody who chooses to drink the Daime sacrament is. There seems to be no clear consensus on the origin of the word religion, but according to scholar Joseph Campbell, it comes from the word *religio*, which means to link back to a source, or to reconnect. The Santo Daime provides an opportunity for everyone in the room to do exactly that. In fact, they appear to be the first church in all of modern history to reconnect their members directly to spirit, not only the privileged few. I know the Catholic Church also serves a sacrament that comes from a different vine, and I understand that not everybody needs to drink a plant medicine to ascend, but you can't convince me that people who swallow a little shot of alcohol and listen to a man read from a book are having the same experience as those drinking Daime, which I find comparable to drinking a living spirit. Weeks after arriving at this conclusion I heard musician Sting make nearly the same statement when he described drinking Ayahuasca in a Brazilian church as the only genuine religious experience he ever had.

Visionary artist Alex Grey speaks about the need to reclaim and reimagine the word religion rather than surrender it to those who have harnessed it for corrupt reasons. He explains that the *primary* religious experience is a mystical experience, and that this is the foundation of all religions. The problems with religion are always secondary, in other words, they are related to all the ensuing structures and rules built up around the original mystical experience. His proposal makes sense, just speaking about the subject always left a nasty taste in my mouth, but why should it? Probably because the word has been hijacked by those in power who use it to divide, spread fear, wage wars and control the masses. I fully support the idea of uniting and reconnecting to spirit. It's probably what the world needs most now, and the new model presented by the Santo Daime is a step in the right direction.

The Santo Daime is currently spreading to other countries around the world and forcing people and governments to re-examine the meaning of the word religion. Another church from Brazil that also consumes Ayahuasca as a sacrament, called the União do Vegetal (UDV), has survived a US Supreme Court decision and the right to practice their faith is now protected by the First Amendment of the Constitution and the Religious Freedom Restoration Act. This precedent may pave the way for the Santo Daime to expand. In fact they have already won legal battles in lower courts in the state of Oregon. Yes, in the country that initiated a worldwide war on drugs it is now possible to drink Ayahuasca, a Schedule One controlled substance according to the Drug Enforcement Agency, in church. I finally appreciated the great work Santo Daime has been doing for the past century. My God, why hadn't I realized this before?

Despite my admiration for the church, which is partly based on Catholicism, I definitely do not claim to be a Christian or a member of the Santo Daime. The necessity to worship Jesus in order to legally drink Ayahuasca for religious purposes is very limiting. After all, why couldn't there be a Buddhist, Hindu, Islamic or Jewish version of the Santo Daime? A Buddhist Daime temple would be a much better match for my style; drink some Daime and then meditate for a few hours. Jesus sounds like an amazing man and a great teacher, but he certainly is not the only path to God.

Our conversation that night inspired me to better know Jesus, so that I could move beyond my distaste for religion and Christianity as it has been presented to me throughout my life. During the next ceremony I respectfully asked the Ayahuasca to show me what some refer to as Christ Consciousness. Norberto had left us a second batch of medicine that was stronger than the Ourinho, and likely contained Jurema. The medicine went deep and it felt like sinking, sinking, sinking into a dark ocean. My mind went silent unlike anything I have ever known and at one point I had an intuition to repeat the phrases:

"The rational mind is no longer dominant over the Higher Self.

The Higher Self is now in control.

The rational mind will take the role of servant to the Higher Self."

In that moment I understood that the rational mind was, and continues to be, a very powerful tool that I respect and appreciate. It is not my enemy. It has protected and helped me over the years, but now it needs to obey the new master.

Repeating those phrases in my head required effort during that strong dose of medicine, as if saying these words was directly related to acting on them. I strained to repeat the words and it felt like physically rewiring a brain that had been operating in a certain pattern for decades. I looked across the other side of the temple and imagined my rational mind "over there," still a part of me, but separate from my true identity. The same concept that people like Adyashanti, Buddha and Eckhart Tolle have been trying to tell us: you are not your mind. Some of us are fortunate enough to have these realizations during ceremony, but the only problem is they can quickly fade when the DMT stops flowing through the system. Now it appears as though I'm learning how to turn this temporary state into a permanent trait, or at least that's the goal. If that's what was happening and I could direct the medicine to help reprogram my human operating system then the implications were incredible. I could progress beyond the same old ceremonial role of passive observer and become a more Active Participant. The idea is very appealing and holds great potential for growth and development. People like Doctors John Lilly and Timothy

Leary have already indicated this is possible with substances like LSD. However, the effects of Ayahuasca can be so powerful (nausea, confusion, fear) that making the transition from observer to participant can be very difficult for many people.

In other words, ceremony for a typical beginner means, buckle your seatbelt and hold on tight, Madre is taking you for a ride. For most people I believe ceremony often looks like this: first you are nervous before drinking the medicine, then you are scared as it takes away control from your mind, fear of death or insanity often occurs, the speed and intensity can feel overwhelming or disorienting, chances are there will be discomfort and nausea, all of this tends to result in resisting the medicine. You may even regret attending the ceremony, promise never to repeat your mistake and pray for it to be finished soon. When the intensity finally decreases many insights emerge, you begin feeling inspired and eventually are eager for more, though some remain shaken for weeks after. The routine is quite common, and a necessary phase for a beginner to endure while they learn to trust and work with the medicine. Norberto once explained how all our lives the mind has been a useful tool that protected us when we needed it most. Because of this we are reluctant to lose it, which is where the resistance comes from. If we can learn to trust the medicine then she shows us something better, the medicine goes deeper and the benefits can be more profound than they already were when we didn't trust it.

Earlier that night we had started by drawing from the tarot deck, and once again the cards spoke to us as if they were alive. I stated my intention to know Christ Consciousness and drew the Tower. Phoenyx shuffled the deck and after stating the same intention she drew the same card. It wasn't only the repetition of cards that fascinated me, but also the appropriateness of the description. Crowley says of the Tower, "Break down the fortress of thine Individual Self, that thy Truth may spring free from the ruins." Quite fitting words for our intentions and what occurred that night. When I repeated the phrases,

"The rational mind is no longer dominant over the Higher Self.

The Higher Self is now in control.

The rational mind will take the role of servant to the Higher Self."

I was basically breaking down the tower of my Individual Self, and could practically feel the ruins created by the destruction of old neural pathways. From this perspective the Truth that sprang free from the ruins was my Higher Self.

Back in chapter one I mentioned the quote, "There must be something more than this," and I think that applies not only to this mundane life, but also to our minds. One of the purposes of Ayahuasca is to show us that there is something more than the mind, something even better, what I call the Higher Self. The question remains as to whether or not I truly attained Christ Consciousness. I expected to have a night full of love and compassion, but that certainly never happened. Instead I entered a deep meditation, free of mind chatter and the usual resistance that accompanies an

Ayahuasca experience. I was introduced to the infinite possibilities available when you learn to cooperate with the medicine and become an Active Participant that has a voice in steering the direction of the ship. It was a practice that I definitely wanted to explore in greater detail during the next ceremony.

Eat Me, Delete Me

During our second stay on the land Norberto had given us another mason jar full of Ayahuasca to share with some other guests who were there that first week. While we had finished one jar during our first visit, we joked that there was no way this would happen again as there were two fewer weeks to accomplish such a feat. The chances of emptying the jar decreased further when the other guests seemed to have absolutely no interest in sitting in ceremony with us. Their last week on the land overlapped with our first week, and as veteran caretakers with far more experience on the property than us, they too had earned the privilege of having the option to drink while Norberto was away. Their refusal to partake reminded us that perhaps the idea of drinking without a shaman present is slightly intimidating. In fact, we too had been reluctant during the first stay, so of course we respected their decision to do what was best for them. I guess they had other priorities, like attending the Santo Daime church, but it was still difficult to imagine passing on this amazing opportunity. We had access to super high quality medicine, a beautiful temple, a pristine environment and a private, peaceful place for resting. On top of that, the Brazilian government classifies Ayahuasca as legal, and other than the plane ticket, it was all free of charge. Considering these factors, where and when would I ever find a better offer to improve myself than here and now? Certainly not in the US where the medicine is illegal and a ceremony typically costs two hundred dollars per night.

We decided to pick up the pace and take full advantage of this unique situation. Instead of the usual three to five days of rest during the first stay, there would only be one to two between ceremonies this time. That fast pace took a toll on our systems, yet it seemed as though something had shifted. Perhaps the medicine was weaker than before, but that was unlikely given Norberto's reputation for cooking strong medicine. The six weeks of Huachuma in Peru must have accelerated the integration process and prepared us for this faster rate of drinking. Or could it be that we had adapted and learned to cooperate with the medicine? Either way, as the end of the visit approached it became apparent that my experiences were much different than before.

During one of the last Juremuasca ceremonies I wished to continue exploring the Active Participation process that I described in the previous chapter. An hour after drinking I felt ill and my first reaction was to pity myself as I thought, "This is horrible, when will it end?" My next step was to try and avoid the discomfort, but then I remembered Norberto's lesson about the four types of feeling. It is important to existentially feel the illness rather than blame others, pity yourself or attach stories. It was necessary to bypass my preprogrammed reactions of self-pity and avoidance, and instead view the situation as an opportunity to improve. So I silently spoke to the plants,

"Yes, Juremuasca, I now understand how you work, this temporary nausea will result in the removal of harmful emotions, energies or toxins stored in my system. Please, continue to clean me. I welcome you inside of me."

Eventually I stepped outside to release a violent purge and felt relief from the illness soon after. To this day I have not yet purged on Huachuma and have only occasionally on Ayahuasca. However, Jurema makes me purge like nothing else is capable of. Probably because the human stomach is not accustomed to eating bark. An alternative explanation is that Jurema behaves like an energetic steel brush and does a great job of cleansing my system. Either way, the silent conversation between the plants and I continued as I experimented with Active Participation:

"The Preto Velho spirit from the Santo Daime Church has instructed me to pray for strength, protection and work. Please grant me this request."

Next, knowing that this South American adventure would eventually come to an end, and a new place to live in the expensive US would be needed, I respectfully asked for:

"Guidance and support in finding a peaceful, healing and affordable home this summer."

Attempting to turn the temporary mystical states of ceremony into permanent traits, I decided to repeat the original phrases from when I first discovered Active Participation:

"The rational mind is no longer dominant over the Higher Self.

The Higher Self is now in control.

The rational mind will take the role of servant to the Higher Self."

And so on, you get the point. I later realized that I was simply using the power of words, prayers and intentions in that powerful expanded state of consciousness to manifest a new reality. Another way of describing it is to say that I was using magic, which brings us back to the *Aleister Crowley Thoth Tarot* cards that we had been drawing at the beginning of each ceremony. Aleister advocated for Practical Magick, a style that includes the use of words to alter physical reality, or as he says, "The science and art of causing change to occur in conformity with Will."

It might not be a coincidence that throughout the winter I often drew the Magus card, otherwise known as the Magician. According to his instruction booklet, the Magus card indicates, "The True Self is the meaning of the True Will: know Thyself through Thy Way." When people hear the word *Will* they might interpret it as a deliberate desire or intention coming from the rational mind. I believe Aleister is capitalizing the word to indicate a desire coming from a higher place. In this case he seems to be saying the True Self and the True Will are equal, as in, your desires or intentions should originate from the True Self *not* the rational mind. In other words, finding *Thy Way* in life, also known as a purpose, depends on connecting to our True Self. I'm not thrilled about the idea of trying to interpret Crowley, a man I barely know who speaks in cryptic language, but perhaps he is offering guidance on how to apply Practical Magick? It sounds like he is saying words carry power and to know whether or not that power is being used ethically our will should come from the True Self since it cannot be corrupted like the rational mind can. That would help explain the Brujos of the Amazon, shamans known to use their powers unethically.

It's difficult to describe that which Aleister calls the True Self, or what I frequently refer to as the Higher Self. For the sake of convenience, and for lack of a better word I sometimes describe the Higher Self as a *state* of consciousness, but I believe that using the term *state* is doing injustice to what would better be described as our True Nature, it is who we always have been, and always will be. While it may be tempting to dismiss this as some flowery, New Age, hippy phrase, the Higher Self is real; in fact, it feels realer than real, concrete and tangible. There's actually nothing *New* about it since many teachers before me have been talking about it for centuries. When I speak of silencing the mind, I may sound like a parrot repeating the phrase of gurus and authors I've previously read, but a silent mind truly is possible to experience during an Ayahuasca journey. For the sake of clarity I should also mention that the term silent mind is not entirely accurate since the mind may continue to chatter. I guess the difference is that the chatter usually decreases, and you can now distinguish between the loud voice of the rational mind versus the quiet voice of the Higher Self. There's no need to believe me, you can always drink a cup to feel it directly and reach your own conclusion. I would LOVE to experience the Higher Self more often *outside* of ceremony. My appreciation for that state of consciousness inspired me to create a mantra with a technological flavor:

"Delete any unnecessary programs and files from my human operating system that prevent me from regularly accessing a higher consciousness during my daily life."

Perhaps my language was the result of watching too many episodes of *Mr. Robot* last summer. Regardless, the mantra felt right at the time, so I used it. Remembering earlier Juremuasca ceremonies when it seemed like the plant spirit was eating unnecessary parts of my mind, I combined the digital and biological processes to create a hybrid. I couldn't avoid smiling as I silently repeated:

"Please Juremuasca, eat me, delete me."

When Norberto returned from his travels, I asked if he had ever heard about the concept of Active Participation. I half expected our expert shaman to reject the idea as some kind of DMT induced fantasy, but instead he knew immediately what I meant. He said that many people fail to recognize the need to participate actively. In the beginning, Madre treats you like a baby and does everything for you, but like any mother she wants you to grow and mature. Many quit drinking the medicine after fifteen to twenty years because she begins to withdraw and the benefits gradually diminish. It's not that she abandons her child; rather a mother can't be expected to continue breastfeeding a teenager. She wants you to eventually cooperate and meet her at least half way. I also asked Norberto whether the reprogramming that I requested is possible. "Yes," he replied, "this is very effective," and then he asked me, "did it work for you?" "I honestly don't know the answer yet," I told him, "and probably will not know until I stop drinking medicine for at least a month." He gave me a big smile and told me to send a WhatsApp when I have the answer. At the rate that we hold ceremony, every time an upgraded version of me is downloaded it gets replaced before I have an opportunity to test the new software. That seems to be the challenge of this adventure, the medicine provided great inspiration for this book, yet I also needed to take a break long enough to determine how much progress was being made. I sought to find a balance between drinking medicine and writing about it. The more I drank, the more material I acquired, which also meant more rest time was needed for my mind to recover from a temporary annihilation, and to regain the clarity to write again. Well, eventually this trip must come to an end, so we'll see what happens then. I promised to let Norberto know in a couple months whether I have become an enlightened master.

People must be skeptical of the Active Participation technique. To simply ask a plant for enlightenment obviously sounds far too easy. In response I would argue that asking is the easy part, but the many steps leading up to the request can be extremely difficult. For a beginner to attend ceremony a single time can be a monumental task complete with terrifying visions, extreme nausea, uncomfortable emotions, painful memories and relived traumas. When you get through all of that, a process that could take years, assuming you have the courage to return a second time, then it is necessary to trust the medicine and lose all resistance. Only when the fear has vanished and the medicine can be invited inside with open arms can the real cooperation begin. To the skeptics I would remind them this process involves much more than to swallow an herbal beverage. Ayahuasca certainly doesn't always go down smoothly. I've known people who vomit within minutes after drinking due to the taste and effect on the stomach. Of course there is also the cost and availability to consider. How many thousands of dollars does it take to reach the stage where it is possible to clearly and confidently be an Active Participant? I don't say these words to discourage, rather to explain that awakening comes at a cost. Ultimately though the benefits of waking from this dream we call life are far greater than the cost, and well worth your effort. Norberto warned that after twenty years of drinking medicine some never learn the process of Active Participation. At the risk of sounding arrogant, I discovered it in only three years, mainly because of this rare opportunity to live on an isolated rainforest property for three months with access to a temple and plenty of medicine. My hope in sharing this concept is that people can learn this process sooner and therefore save money and accelerate their development.

The Fountain

One of the most important questions many writers must answer is probably, how does it end? This reminds me of scenes from the artistic movie *The Fountain* starring Hugh Jackman, when the dying wife asks her husband to finish writing the book that she has nearly completed and he replies, "But I don't know how it ends." Her story about a Spanish conquistador searching for the Tree of Life in Central America includes a description of a dying star called Xibalba, which represents the underworld to the Mayan people, who believe their souls go there after death. The fearful and angry husband views death as an enemy that he vows to defeat to avenge the loss of his wife. This incredibly underrated movie ends with him accepting his mortality and then floating up to Xibalba before bursting into light and ecstasy as he reunites with the Great Beyond. The look of pure bliss on his face makes the audience wonder why he was fighting against death all these years.

I always assumed this book would end in a similar way with a big bang like the grand finale at a Fourth of July fireworks display. In that scenario I would drink a large cup of super potent Ayahuasca and then undergo an ego death and ascend straight up to the stars. Truth be told, the way this Brazilian adventure actually ended was quite unexpected, as it always is with Ayahuasca. There was no grand finale, in fact it was very peaceful, yet equally spectacular and definitely worth sharing. Any book is obviously easier for an author to finish when there is an exciting climax to write about, so the challenge I face here is convincing you how profound my last ceremony actually was. Don't get the wrong impression, it wasn't through lack of effort that there was no big bang; in fact we were drinking doses that would probably blast many people out of the solar system. Despite the absence of fireworks it was a major accomplishment that signaled a graduation to the next level.

Phoenyx and I were perplexed about the mild reactions we were having from the medicine, which Norberto had told us was the same kind of Ayahuasca (Ourinho) that we had started with. Four months earlier during our first stay on the land a hundred milliliters pushed me near my limits and resulted in purging, discomfort and frequent glances at the phone to estimate how much longer until the intensity would decrease. This time around we were more curious to know how a powerful experience had been reduced to such a mild one. Not that I couldn't feel anything, but it was more of a dreamy state than anything else. Of course there are people who would view our doses as mild in comparison to what they take. Human nature is to always strive for bigger, faster, higher and longer no matter what the activity is.

Terence McKenna famously coined the phrase *heroic dose*, a reference to taking the threshold dose of five-dried grams needed to have a complete breakthrough with Psilocybin Mushrooms. In recent times Kilindi Iyi has far surpassed this weight by venturing into the realms of forty grams. There are occasionally people who feel nothing after drinking a standard size shot of Ayahuasca. Phoenyx once saw a woman down an entire *glass* without effect. There's no clear explanation of why this happens. Perhaps they are resistant, or it's somehow related to their biochemistry. In stark contrast, Norberto admits to barely drinking at all these days. Just a mere drop or sip is all he needs to get into alignment with the task at hand, monitoring forty participants simultaneously to ensure everyone's safety. He's not the first person to tell me this. Recently our favorite Huachumero in Peru told me that the longer you drink the less you need to feel a connection with the plant.

Regardless, the final ceremony left me wondering if this was a different batch than the previous jar we had finished during the first stay after all? Before asking Norberto for his expert opinion of the situation, Phoenyx and I developed a list of some possible explanations for our peaceful achievement. We thought that if one learns to trust the medicine, this strange and foreign intelligence, then fear, resistance and the resulting drama might disappear. Or perhaps we began to vibrate at the same frequency as the Ourinho, to come into resonance and therefore harmony with it? Did the Ourinho slowly break through blockages that had earlier prevented the heart from opening to feel her gentle, soft, caring, feminine energy? Could it be that when the blockages are cleared and you align with the medicine, energy flows more freely through the body without turbulence and the resulting confusion and discomfort?

Norberto later confirmed that the first and second mason jars each came from the same source. A jar filled from the bottom of the pot could be stronger than one filled from the top due to the particles that settle, regardless, the source had not changed. That led to the ultimate conclusion, if the medicine was the same then *we* must have changed. Of course anybody would after drinking seventeen times, including seven out of the past seventeen days. That is to be expected, but I didn't realize my personal transformation would result in a radical shift in how I experienced the medicine. Norberto described the way Ayahuasca peels off unnecessary layers from our minds like an onion, just the right amount, not too little, not too much. He also mentioned how gentle she can usually be after the main work is complete, as if she somehow knows how long the workshop is, and when to come to closure. In this case, we were reaching the end of what was essentially a three-month workshop and Madre was satisfied with the progress we made, so she was now ready to show us her sweet side. Chances are that I may struggle at the beginning of the next workshop as the peeling process begins once again, but until then I could enjoy this motherly embrace.

My first time attending one of Norberto's three-day workshops matched this description. Madre didn't waste any time peeling my onion layers. The first day is usually an introduction to the medicine, when Norberto serves a lighter batch to the group. On the second day a majority of the difficult work is done, this is when he brings the strong stuff. Barely thirty minutes into the second ceremony and I released an epic purge in the form of an *Incredible Hulk* yell, as mentioned in the previous chapter. Shortly after I was declaring to Phoenyx that, "Even if nothing happens the remainder of this weekend, my work here is done." I intuitively knew that the main reason for attending that workshop was already complete, and as evidence for this the third day was quite gentle and free of discomfort.

Back to the final ceremony, at one point in the evening I took advantage of the peace to express my gratitude to Ourinho for the amazing opportunity to be invited as caretaker for the land, which generated all the material and inspiration for writing this book. I then asked if there was anything she would like to add. While there was not an audible answer, shortly after my question the concept of this chapter entered my awareness. I thought about sitting up right then and there to type the words that appeared, but three hours after drinking I was peaking and decided not to risk missing any other insights that might emerge. Instead I waited a few more hours to type the first paragraph to this chapter. Who knew that one could type coherent paragraphs under the influence of Ayahuasca?! In fact, the clarity that can be achieved during ceremony is incredible and stands in opposition to false impressions people have of intoxicating drugs that leave us hallucinating and confused. I probably wouldn't attempt to prepare my yearly taxes or drive a car after drinking the medicine, but I trust my intuition and ability to discern equally, if not more than when I am sober. Although I never literally hear voices, this book seems to be written at least half by Madre Ayahuasca and half by me, not to forget the assistance received from Grandfather

Huachuma. Nearly every time I sat down to type, it had only been between one to five days since I last drank him or her, so they were always in my system. Because plants don't have fingers to type I often felt like their ambassador, a messenger acting as a bridge between this dimension and the next.

While I never ascended to Xibalba in an ecstatic flash of brilliant light, I did make peace with Madre Ayahuasca. That alone is a major victory for me. I realized that my greatest fear (death) is actually what I should be pursuing rather than avoiding. Death of the rational mind, death of that which no longer serves me, and preparation for the inevitable death of the body. Sacred Medicines teach us to face our fears, which is the first step to dissolving them. Our fears limit us, but once we come to peace with them, doors open and a new sense of freedom becomes accessible. I can say all the right words here, but I guess the true test comes the next time I drink a potent cup of Ayahuasca, or the ultimate test when I leave this physical world behind. In the movie *Doctor Strange*, The Ancient One says at the end of her centuries-long life, "You'd think after all this time I'd be ready, but look at me stretching one moment out into a thousand just so I can watch the snow."

Well, that concludes our three months in Brazil. It is now that time when we slowly stand up, if you are able to, take your time, and hold your neighbors' hands while we recite the closing prayer:

The Fountain

Life

Health

Happiness

Open paths

Health in the body

Peace in the spirit

And love in the heart

It is this that we wish

For ourselves

For our loved ones

And for all of our brothers and sisters

So be it

And with these words and this prayer in our hearts, the ceremony (and this section of the book) is now closed!!!

☿

After Brazil

To Serve in Peru

For the second time in two months we needed to say goodbye to Brazil. I was feeling reluctant to leave, and wondered if our services would ever be needed again. Sure there would always be the opportunity to return and attend a ten-day workshop on the land, but after living here free of charge for three months, the thought of paying to stay for a limited time was difficult for me to accept. The greatest benefits seem to come from an extended experience. Besides, I liked being the caretaker. My concerns were quickly relieved during the bumpy ride Norberto gave us down to the bus stop on the day of departure. Minutes before the bus arrived he revealed a few things that we were surprised to learn. For one, of all the caretakers who watched the property over the years nobody had stayed continually on the land without a break for as long as we did. During the first seven weeks we left for one single day down to the nearby village, and during the second five weeks we only left for a single overnight visit to the Santo Daime church. Even more surprising was to learn that no caretaker had ever drunk Ayahuasca alone before. We assumed that everybody was left a large bottle to drink as part of the exchange, in addition to the food and lodging that was included in the deal. Again, Norberto made this decision after many years of observing Phoenyx in ceremony, both as a participant, and as an assistant. Not only had we been the first to drink, but we finished a full liter both times, and had even asked for more. If Ayahuasca drinking were an event at the Spiritual Olympics then we just won the gold medal. This obviously is not a competition, but my ego must not have been completely annihilated as I still felt a sense of pride about our accomplishments. Seriously though, I believe that Norberto views our feats as a symbol of our appreciation for his land, and the medicine that he cooks. Quite similar to the way a chef would enjoy watching a customer lick the plate clean following a delicious meal. When Phoenyx told him that I was sad about leaving that final morning, he replied, "Good, this is a compliment for me!" Any tears I might have had quickly evaporated when Norberto invited us to return as caretakers as soon as Brazilian Visa regulations allowed. In that moment I had a vision of the future and knew we would return for another adventure the following winter. I also knew that we had done an excellent job serving as caretakers since otherwise he wouldn't invite us back. This is ultimately what I wanted, for him to appreciate us as much as we appreciated the amazing opportunity he provided.

Our next step was to fly to Peru for a second round of Huachuma (San Pedro) integration. I felt like a tennis ball bouncing back and forth across the continent, Atlantic to Pacific Ocean, Brazil to Peru, and repeat. The second trip to that little Andean town that I call Kamar-Taj was even better than the first. On the drive there from the airport I wondered exactly why we were returning instead of flying home to the US. I told Phoenyx we better keep our eyes wide open because eventually our purpose for being there would be revealed. It soon became apparent that even with our eyes closed it would have been impossible to miss our purpose for being there. The blessings continued to shower down upon us, first we found a peaceful place to stay outside of town, further away from the barking dogs, late night celebrations and busy town energy. It was the perfect location to hold private Huachuma ceremonies, and continue working on this book. I had a panoramic view of the valley from my writing desk that was inspirational to say the least. I also reached an agreement with a local artist to design the image for the cover of this book. Not only did I admire her work, she was also the person who made the psychedelic poster that drew me into the full moon party where I first met Phoenyx three years ago, so it seemed fitting that she would join the team to be part of this creative process. To top it off, we didn't get Giardia this time either.

A major highlight of the second visit was to finally attend a full moon ceremony with our favorite Huachumero, something that never happened during the first visit despite our best intentions and efforts. Following three months of drinking Ayahuasca in Brazil without the presence of a facilitator we had grown quite accustomed to drinking alone. Practically speaking, it was also much more affordable, so the incentive to drink with others was shrinking. However, we still recognize the benefits of paying a facilitator who has much to offer, as was the case with this Huachumero. Around mid-afternoon we followed him on a path that led out of town up into the mountains and walked to his small property. With the exception of some wire fencing and a flat landing pad carved out of the steep terrain, the land is undeveloped and you would never see it unless you knew where to look. In addition to the fence surrounding the property, the land is also protected by small San Pedro cacti hiding in the grasses along the perimeter every meter or two. After he set up the altar our small group of six participants began ceremony near sunset. We each started with a third of a liter and then settled in for a long night of whatever was to come. A fire was lit to warm us through the cool Andean night, and kept burning until sunrise. One of the participants drinking for her first time aggressively purged only an hour after drinking. For some reason I still have not purged on Huachuma, but welcome the opportunity to be cleansed someday. After her release I spent much of the night answering her questions about Sacred Medicines. Although she would probably never admit it, talking to another person is a great strategy for surviving a challenging Huachuma experience. As I mentioned in the previous Peru chapter, the problem is that you then avoid internal work that needs attention. While I enjoy discussing my favorite subject, I too missed the opportunity to look within. One thing I didn't miss was the big, bright, beautiful full moon shining overhead.

The most memorable lesson I learned from our Huachumero that night was his preferred method of cooking medicine. It is common to either cook or compost the head, the top part of the cactus, but judging by his passionate opinion, this was a great mistake. When the head is instead replanted, the cactus can then continue living, which allows the consumer to drink an actual living spirit. On the other hand, throwing the head onto the compost pile to decay is like an insult, a waste of medicine and a lack of respect for all the plant has to offer.

It's almost an injustice to reduce this second six week trip to Peru and a series of Huachuma ceremonies to a single chapter in this book once again, but the focus here is Brazil and Ayahuasca, so a more detailed story about the Grandfather cactus will need to wait until later. After all, Huachuma deserves an entire book, not just a couple chapters. When I told our Huachumero that the subject of my next book could possibly be Huachuma, he replied that this cactus requires not only an entire book, but many lifetimes to be understood. Even that might not be enough because the cactus itself is not static and continues to evolve. It was a humbling reminder that I am merely a writer sharing my opinions and observations with those who are curious, and while I may know much more than the average person, I'm definitely not an expert. In fact, when it comes to this divine plant, who really is? Regardless, it was clear to me that this relatively unknown Sacred Medicine deserves more attention than it was currently receiving. Despite a wave of new data washing over society from the emergence of the so-called Psychedelic Renaissance, research of San Pedro as a medicine has been ignored. Scientists were studying LSD, MDMA, Ayahuasca and Psilocybin, but not Mescaline or the plant from which it comes. Perhaps I could shine some light on the subject?

One of the more funny moments occurred the following week during a Huachuma ceremony at our house overlooking the valley. We set a blanket out in the tall grass and enjoyed an amazing view of the surrounding Apus that soared above us. According to folklore the mountains have spirits known as Apus that are believed to protect inhabitants of the region. As I stared at the Apu across the valley, Phoenyx got inspired to take a photo. The end result was an excellent photo of me sitting in meditation pose with a wool blanket wrapped around my body and a look of peace on my face. I soon became aware that she was taking my photo, but at no point did I ever change my position or expression. She simply captured the moment and commented on how I appeared to be "Now-ing," a reference to Eckhart Tolle. This photo became one of my favorites, mostly because I looked great without the need to pose for the camera. A few days later I realized that many of my Instagram followers had never seen what I look like and decided that photo would be a great introduction to the man behind the SacredMedicineGuide user name. I inserted a few hashtags like #meditation, #powerofnow and #ultraspiritual. The last being a reference to comedian philosopher JP Sears who likes to remind people in the spiritual community not to take themselves too seriously. I had recently been more confident while facing fears about openly sharing my psychedelic experiences, but in this case I saw no need to mention them in the post. To my surprise and amusement I later received a notification from Instagram saying that Eckhart Tolle liked my photo. Judging by the quarter million followers the account had I was quite certain it was truly him, or at least one of his assistants who he trusts enough to represent him. Either way, Eckhart Tolle likes a photo of me meditating on a strong dose of Huachuma.

We also drank medicine with an Australian friend walking a very similar path as mine, who prior to that visit had been an online acquaintance that I never met in person. It was a great opportunity to share ideas and hear his perspective on being a pioneer in the field of Sacred Medicine. We were both attempting to transition from the old paradigm to a new one where we earn an income by helping people truly transform their lives, but we weren't fully there yet. Which business practices should be adopted in the new paradigm? For me it's essential to carefully navigate the relationship between money and spirituality while acknowledging that some kind of equal exchange for services provided is still necessary. At what point is one ready to serve customers, and how far should one go to draw them? Introducing Sacred Medicines to less experienced people is a great responsibility and I think serious self-inquiry and maturity are required before anybody decides to walk down this path. Our conversations helped me to learn what parts of his style I wanted to adopt versus those I would rather avoid.

The biggest highlight of the visit occurred on the last day in Peru. While receiving a massage from an American who has been living in the area for many years, Phoenyx was invited to begin serving Ayahuasca on her next trip to Peru. The request was particularly meaningful because this therapist has his fingers firmly placed on the pulse of the local medicine community due to all the people he sees each day. Having a schedule that is frequently full of clients and more than an hour to thoroughly speak with each of them, he has a keen sense of what's happening around town. In this case there is already a well-known and respected man available who has been serving Ayahuasca to locals and visitors for many years. The only problem is his ceremonies can be quite large which means that the more challenged participants can't always get the extra attention they need. Ultimately the relationship is between the medicine and the participant, but when people are struggling with a difficult condition such as treatment-resistant Post Traumatic Stress Disorder (PTSD) it certainly helps to have a facilitator or assistant available to provide additional support.

While it rarely happens around this town, stories of inappropriate behavior between influential male shamans and vulnerable female participants are more common down in the Amazon Rainforest. There is a general shortage of females capable of serving medicine, so when a woman comes in for a massage and asks for advice on where to attend ceremony, not many options exist. Since this therapist has been massaging Phoenyx for years and has also sat with her in ceremony, he is well aware of her experience level working with the medicine, the obstacles she overcame and her original reasons for seeking Ayahuasca. Probably the most important factor in his decision to invite her to serve though was hearing the story of what we were doing in Brazil that winter. You could say that living for three months as caretakers of an isolated rainforest property and drinking two liters of Ayahuasca without any supervision was a type of initiation or rite of passage. The beauty of it being that the initiation was not planned, and there was never an intention to serve medicine when the trip was finished.

The funny thing about the therapist's invitation was that a recurring topic of conversation for us while spending time in Kamar-Taj was, when is a person ready to serve? A quick walk around town reveals numerous posters taped to café windows advertising ceremonies. When reading these posters and considering whether or not to choose a facilitator it's important to ask the question, why does this person feel qualified to serve? Some are in it for the money. Others claim the plant spirit directly told them they are ready. Occasionally, and alarmingly, there are people who declare after their first ceremony that they heard the calling, and proceed to find customers soon after. Since there are no agencies passing out shaman licenses, anybody can serve medicine, but should they? Phoenyx wondered if it is necessary to first work as an apprentice, or can the plant directly teach you everything you need to know? I guess the therapist thought her time spent as an assistant for Norberto was adequate. What I find most appealing about Phoenyx's invitation is that the request came from an outside source. There were no inner delusions or suspicious motives involved. She is debt free and not seeking a quick source of income. She is a heterosexual woman so there is no risk of using her power to take advantage of unsuspecting female participants. She has been drinking Ayahuasca for years so there is no shortage of experience to draw from. She has overcome her own traumas and now has the ability to relate to others who come from a similar background. She has cleaned the purge buckets as an assistant for Norberto and knows that the work is not always pretty. And once again she survived the initiation without freaking out, setting the temple on fire and running away naked through the rainforest. There's nothing wrong with a little freak out, but you probably don't want it to happen to your facilitator. Above all, she was unexpectedly selected by a veteran from the community, similar to how Norberto reluctantly began serving after his mentor Baixinha encouraged him to step up to the next level.

Another benefit of being selected by your community is that it's not necessary to aggressively advertise and play the competitive capitalistic game of always trying to persuade people to choose you by posting on social media every day. Instead customers come through referrals and word of mouth. Your reputation and the high quality of work you do brings both new and return participants. You are simply filling an existing need, or providing a supply for the healing that people demand. Or at least we hope this is the case, but who knows, it may take some time for people to recognize what we have to offer. The advantages of Norberto's style need to be experienced directly. Talking about it is simply not enough. Phoenyx's invitation means I may have an opportunity to serve as her assistant should she decide to accept the offer. Perhaps I can also be an assistant at one of Norberto's workshops. I guess after receiving all these healings, teachings and blessings it almost feels like an obligation for us to provide a safe space, so others have the opportunity to receive them as well.

Home

After nearly six months in Brazil and Peru it was time to begin preparing for a trip to the United States. Besides practical factors such as tourist Visa limitations, there were many enticing reasons to return to my adopted homeland, the Pacific Northwest. It was late spring and despite the region's reputation as being a dark and wet place, the weather there is usually unsurpassed during the summer season. While the rest of the country gets punished with heat waves and destructive storms, the Pacific Northwest is often pleasantly warm and mostly dry, the perfect conditions for backpacking through the many National Parks and designated wilderness areas in that region. In addition to the climate, a trip back home can be summarized in two words: comfort and convenience. As much as I love Brazil and Peru, the thought of sleeping on my natural-rubber-latex mattress, without dogs barking all night or town fiestas lasting until two in the morning, was beckoning me. Our list of movies we wanted to watch on my big-screen TV was growing. I looked forward to the high-speed internet, full-sized keyboard and trackpad that would make writing much easier than the iPad I was currently using. Hot showers with high pressure sounded like heaven compared to the warm trickle we often found in Peru. A car to come and go as I pleased would be an added luxury. The simple pleasures in life. One of the greatest benefits of world travel is the renewed appreciation for the privileges we have that are often taken for granted.

In the "Eat Me, Delete Me" chapter I described the process of Active Participation, similar to praying for what we want or need in life. During the ceremony featured there I had requested:

"Guidance and support in finding a peaceful, healing and affordable home this summer."

Around the exact same time Phoenyx and I began discussing plans for our departure I unexpectedly received a message from my former roommate asking if I wanted to return to the place I had lived last year. It was yet another synchronicity in a long list that we experienced over the winter. Finding an apartment while you are thousands of miles away is not always easy, and most property managers request a one-year lease, which is a commitment that definitely does not match my lifestyle. The roommate that she had replaced me with back in the "Evicted" chapter was now ready to move out, so once again we could swap positions as I replaced him. Like I said earlier, there were never any major problems between us, she simply wanted to live with a close friend, and our agreement was only month to month. I just assumed she would never invite me back because as a vegetarian she sometimes complained about the smells produced by my Paleo-Ayurveda diet, like bone broth from the crockpot, or grass-fed beef frying on the stovetop. However, she was away traveling a great majority of the time, so if I timed the crockpot cooking accordingly there shouldn't be any conflicts. I'd love to eat vegetarian more often, but try and understand that I'm allergic to a majority of the vegetarian diet. The apartment is located only a couple blocks from a nice forested park that is the perfect spot for a Rapé session, and the organic food cooperative is not much further away, so driving is rarely necessary. The living situation certainly met my qualifications of being "peaceful, healing and affordable," and it manifested effortlessly, so I accepted her offer.

Phoenyx decided to stop at Lake Tahoe on the way to Washington to attend a week-long Adyashanti silent meditation retreat, or nearly silent as participants are allowed to ask the Zen teacher questions in the evening. She is well aware of my love for the Terence McKenna quote, "Avoid gurus, follow plants," and she mostly agrees, but also believes the two can be combined for maximum effectiveness. Don't blindly follow a guru, she suggests, instead drink Sacred Medicines and then let the guru help you transform the temporary states of ceremony into permanent traits of daily living. Unfortunately Adya admits to never having consumed Ayahuasca before. Now that would be a potent fusion, a Zen master meeting a master plant. A true test to see how advanced he actually is. During the question and answer session Adya could not deny the healing power of Ayahuasca to help people suffering from treatment-resistant psychological conditions. This concession is very important because even though meditation can be a valuable addition to your daily routine, the benefits can be elusive to those constantly triggered by their condition. Despite his chemical-free approach, he did estimate that around *half* of his students have pursued his teachings only after *first* being introduced to Sacred Medicines.

Phoenyx tells a funny story she once heard of a different Zen master drinking Ayahuasca for his first time in Peru. A couple hours into ceremony and he completely fell apart, a total mess on display while some of his devout students watched in disbelief. There is absolutely nothing wrong with falling apart, in fact I encourage people to do so. Shatter all your illusions and crush your beliefs that you have the universe figured out. The arrogance of thinking we know all the answers is the source of many of our problems. Yet the story illustrates a common deficiency I see in the spiritual community, those who discriminate against plant medicines, which in my humble opinion should disqualify most of them from wearing whatever title they carry. This is a subject I will elaborate on in the final chapter. A Zen master who can be in peace with whatever comes up during a strong Ayahuasca ceremony is one who definitely catches my attention because they have tested their practice against a plant that pushes the mind beyond ordinary limits. Anyway, I would have liked to meet Adya, but decided to go straight to Bellingham in order to conserve my dwindling savings account.

When Phoenyx finally arrived in Washington, we wasted no time in following the instructions of the Preto Velho spirit from the Santo Daime church. To eliminate my food allergies she had told me, "Go to church and bathe in the ocean seven times; pray for 'strength, protection and work.'" As strange as it sounded I was absolutely willing to try. Phoenyx and I attended seven different churches in two months, including: Unitarian, Catholic, Presbyterian, Lutheran, Methodist and Greek Orthodox denominations. There were no Islamic mosques nearby, so to top it off we visited the Jewish synagogue. I'm not a religious guy, so the experience was a bit awkward, although the people were always very kind and welcoming. Many times they assumed we were new members of the community and asked questions about what brought us there. "Uhh, I took psychedelic drugs at a church in Brazil and the spirit of an African slave told me that coming here would relieve my food allergies," I wanted to say. As entertaining as their response might have been, I politely told them we were exploring their church and tried to avoid the subject as much as possible. They always seemed so excited to have potential new members join, and I can see why. Composed mostly of elderly people, churches seem to be struggling to survive, at least in the progressive university town I was living in. The only time we ever saw younger people was when parents brought their children along. I'm not surprised, the standard Christian service was so incredibly different from the Santo Daime experience, which featured a much younger congregation. Don't get me wrong, they're trying, they truly are, but Sacred Medicines best connect me to God. You could argue that we're always connected to God. In response I would say that Sacred Medicines make me more aware of that link. It's not just faith, it's a deep knowing. At some point during each service I found an opportunity to pray for "strength, protection and work." Lucky for me, I live on the West Coast, so salt water is never too far away. After church we went to the local bay in Puget Sound and bathed in the cold water while I again prayed for "strength, protection and work."

Throughout the summer I continued to downsize my possessions. Prior to my first trip to Peru I had decided to rent a storage unit for all my stuff. Three years later with no signs of settling down in sight I wanted to let go of anything that wasn't necessary to keep. With the help of a dear friend who generously allowed me to store a few furniture items in her basement, I moved out of a fifteen by five foot unit and can now easily fit inside a four by four. I've noticed how in our society people attempt to buy their way to happiness through the never ending accumulation of material items. It's funny because I experience the opposite. Every time I sell, donate or recycle more of my stuff, I feel better afterwards. In a similar way that people have a sense of accomplishment from finding a discount price, I too have that sense when somebody stops by to purchase an item I posted on Craigslist. I feel lightness, mobility and freedom. Having moved across the country many times, I like knowing that the next move will be an easier one than the last. In the pursuit of personal growth, my possessions can be like magnets that pull me back and constantly remind me of earlier versions of myself. Sometimes it's difficult to release our belongings and the memories attached to them. Perhaps the rational mind identifies with these things and selling them feels like selling ourselves? Ultimately I think it's healthy to live in the present. "What if I need it later, what if I settle down or what if I regret selling it?" These thoughts often pass through my mind, but if I haven't used it in three years then chances are it can go.

Downsizing is also a step towards sustainability, consuming less of the planet's precious resources by focusing on what we truly need. Don't get me wrong, I'm not a total ascetic. I still own things that I want, or because they bring me pleasure. I guess the distinguishing factor is that I truly appreciate these items. The mantra is, quality not quantity. Buying fewer things allows me to ration my hard-earned money, and spend it on experiences instead, like traveling to South America where for six months of the year I live with only a backpack! Travel reminds me there are few things I actually need to survive or be happy. I invite you to consider that as you walk through your home. A cluttered home clutters the mind. Our minds are already at full capacity, let's simplify our surroundings so we can clear our minds. Do you know exactly where everything is at all times? I do, because there are not too many places it could hide in a four by four foot storage space. The government tax collectors won't like this message. Corporate advertisers don't want you to listen to me either. Never-ending economic growth they say. Consume, consume, consume. You don't want to be out of style. Got to have the newest version every year if you want acceptance. "Why?" I say, "You are not your car!" Use your stuff until it stops working, until it has holes, until it can't be repaired anymore. And if you are ready to upgrade before it breaks then find a new home for it, there's always somebody in need. I can't tell you how many times I see people putting completely functioning items in the garbage.

Come on people, it's time to Wake Up, we can do this! We're walking down a path towards a spiritual desert. Let's replace consumerism with minimalism. Can't we just go to the lake without a speed boat or jet ski? Isn't it possible to enjoy the peaceful forest without a snowmobile, motor bike or four wheeler? You wouldn't need to work the overtime necessary to pay for the big truck that pulls all the toys, or the gas that fuels them. Actually, new trends are emerging, look at the idea of tiny homes for an example. I'm not sure if this represents an awakening or simply the rising costs of living in the US. Either way, spirituality is slowly coming back to take its rightful place alongside materialism. Why choose one when we could have both? Having an abundance of physical items in a soulless society isn't very appealing, but for most people neither is meditating in a cave all day. In the movie *Black Panther* we see an example of the Wakanda people harnessing advanced technology while still maintaining their ceremonial traditions, following a moral compass and living in harmony with the environment.

To make that transition a new understanding of life is needed. Inventor and pioneer Nikola Tesla once said, "If you want to find the secrets of the universe, think in terms of energy, frequency and vibration." He seems to be directing us beyond the everyday realm of three dimensions, and to focus instead upon a reality that is not easily perceived with our ordinary senses.

We enjoyed the comfort and convenience that my few remaining physical possessions had to offer. It was a perfect opportunity to integrate the many ceremonies we had the good fortune to participate in last winter. High-quality, nutrient-dense food; plenty of rest; hiking and camping; along with crossing some entertaining movies off our list were exactly what we needed. Phoenyx was introduced to my favorite band Phish, arguably the best improvisational live musicians of all time, at the Gorge Amphitheater. The Gorge offers a stunning, wide-open view of the Columbia River directly behind the stage. Psychedelics are notoriously present at Phish concerts, though they are typically consumed in a more recreational manner. Don't expect to see a circle of people holding hands to chant an opening prayer before the band comes onstage. Having said that, I do think it's possible to respectfully experience Sacred Medicines in a more social setting. However, it does require a greater level of maturity to deal with the additional scenarios arising that wouldn't normally be found in the safe space inside a temple. Some people are there to simply party, while others are having legitimate spiritual awakenings with the assistance of amazing music and a spectacular light show. My psychedelic history has come full circle. The live-music scene introduced me to these substances as a teenager, though back then I never referred to them as Sacred Medicines. I didn't understand the concept and nobody ever explained it to me until I reached my late thirties. As a teen psychedelics were mostly used for fun and exploration. Regardless, I'm certain they expanded my consciousness, whether that was my intention or not. Twenty years later and I'm learning to combine the recreational with the medicinal in an exciting and responsible way, the best of both worlds.

I was initially hesitant to share this last paragraph for fear of being labeled. I didn't want to give the wrong impression, but then realized that if I haven't convinced you by now of the important role Sacred Medicines play in my life, and the potential they have to heal individuals and help humanity, then I never will. You see, psychedelics have been carrying a lot of baggage since the 1960s. They are associated with hippies, unproductive members of society who only want to get high. Yes, that is one possibility, among many others. People say the sixties were a failed experiment, the first large scale introduction of Sacred Medicine to the Modern Mind. The sixties didn't fail, it was intentionally crushed, under the heel of a government, and the corporations influencing it, who saw expanded consciousness as a major threat to capitalism, and their ability to manipulate the masses. Mind control is quite easy when you take away the number one tool for opening the mind. People often blame Timothy Leary for the so-called sixties failure. He took a lot of shit, but from what I could see his intentions were pure. I don't think he ever intended to do harm; quite the opposite in fact. Evidence indicates he was the prize target in an attempt to discredit a peaceful revolution using every means available. He was sentenced to excessively long prison terms for tiny amounts of Cannabis on two separate incidents. We should be honoring this pioneer, not blaming him. Sure, mistakes were made, but lessons were also learned. What do you expect? We didn't have shamans or wise elders guiding us.

Admittedly, I wasn't even alive during the sixties. Perhaps I'm not qualified to be an expert on the subject since I wasn't physically present, but I'm at least entitled to an opinion, especially considering that the consequences of that decade continue to affect me even to this day, for better and worse. My impression of those years is of a situation that appeared very wild at times. Naked people spinning in circles and dancing ecstatically in the middle of Golden Gate Park. Perhaps it was a natural reaction to the more controlled and orderly years preceding them as the pendulum swung back in the opposite direction. Honestly, I can see both sides, why the youth were rebelling and why the mainstream was fearful of this radical change. I guess as a society we were not ready yet. To speak the language of the transformational coaching program I completed last summer, there was a lack of preparation by those who participated in their first psychedelic experiences, and probably a lack of integration afterwards. Regardless, the government's reaction was extreme, and the ensuing drug prohibitions resulted in decades of lost research as both recreational and medicinal use were locked down.

In *Fear and Loathing in Las Vegas*, Hunter S. Thompson wrote of the sixties, "We had all the momentum. We were riding the crest of a high and beautiful wave…" Well, the wave finally broke, but it's now building once again. During the second attempt, this current Psychedelic Renaissance of scientific research following a forty-year drought, everybody wants to get it right. Let's not screw up this time, advocates say. It's true, we need access to Sacred Medicines now more than ever and can't afford any errors or public relations disasters. We must be as professional and scientific as possible to persuade the mainstream to accept these substances. Hedonistic over indulgers like Thompson probably should not be our spokesperson. But we also need to be honest. The joy that can come from an experience will be as equally influential to the public as the healing. It sure as hell tops any whiskey buzz I ever had, by a thousand. Have you ever heard Jimi Hendrix play *Bold as Love* during the peak of an Ayahuasca ceremony? I highly recommend it, like an orgasm of sonic rainbows cascading from his guitar. The sixties didn't fail me, I find them to be inspirational. All of the radical personalities, political movements and art from that time period that warned me of the dangers of conformity. Their message carries on like ripples across time. That's the thing, the Sacred can't be hidden, at least not permanently or completely. It always finds a way to re-enter our lives.

As the summer passed Phoenyx's Visa eventually expired, so she moved on to Europe; our first separation in nearly nine months. I was alone now and needed to follow the Preto Velho's instructions without her assistance. If you can remember, to complete my mission I needed to perform a ritual and offer the foods that trigger my reactions back to the ocean. For this task I thought it would be best to do it in style. Rather than visiting the heavily populated Puget Sound I would make a road trip to the Olympic National Park where there are miles of wilderness coastline accessible only by foot, a rare occurrence considering nearly all of the East Coast is highly developed, and a great majority of the West Coast at least has a road nearby. I backpacked to a camping site four miles from the car, far enough to only see a few people over the next three days. I built an altar in the sand and placed a pot full of legumes, seeds, nuts and grains in the middle. A small chunk of cheese sat on top. All alone in the wilderness, I had quite a powerful ceremony that day. In fact, it was so intense that I literally got on my hands and knees to pray for mercy. If you want to know what kind of medicine was served at this ceremony then you will have to use your imagination. In the weeks that followed I would slowly reintroduce these foods back into my diet and see what happens. Having practiced a strict diet for nearly four years I barely missed my old diet anymore, but it would be nice to have more options if this protocol worked.

Somewhere along the way Norberto invited us back for the coming winter, and we happily accepted his offer. Since we were going to Brazil, we might as well cross the border to visit Peru again. Phoenyx was now strongly considering to serve medicine as a facilitator for the first time, and I agreed to assist. Let's at least try and see how it goes, we decided. If the participants appreciate our work and receive relief from their suffering then we will continue. A new pattern was emerging, US and Europe during summer, Brazil and Peru during winter. Apparently psychedelics dissolve not only our conditioned beliefs, but also national boundaries. The rational mind may identify with the state or country it's born in, but we're all citizens of Earth. It looks like the beginning of a global lifestyle. The internet and a new generation of mobile devices allow us to bring the office wherever we go. Crypto coins have the potential to provide a form of payment that doesn't need conversion to the local currency. Downsizing gives us the freedom to go where we choose. Caretaking and house-sharing services make it easier to find a temporary home without living in a hotel or signing a lease.

A question that naturally arises is, where is home for me these days? I was born and raised in Minneapolis, Minnesota, but have spent most of the past fifteen years in the Pacific Northwest after discovering the wilderness, progressive values and health-conscious living that the region is known for. Now even that is changing as I spend more time on the road. It still feels necessary to have a base for resting and to integrate my journeys, yet at my current rate of downsizing that four by four foot storage unit will soon shrink to zero. To answer the question, I no longer have a home, instead I have many homes. Or perhaps it's better not to define a geographic location. Ultimately, our home is an infinite Universe. If you are flexible enough to adopt that perspective then I guess you can find peace wherever you go.

"In the province of the mind, what one believes to be true is true or becomes true, within certain limits to be found experientially and experimentally. These limits are further beliefs to be transcended. In the mind, there are no limits."

-Dr. John Lilly, inventor of the sensory isolation tank

Catalyzing Consciousness

Many people come to Ayahuasca in search of healing, or to be more accurate, to find relief from their suffering. Imagine how uncomfortable their daily existence must be to pursue a plant brew that is classified as illegal around much of the planet, and to explore systems of medicine that come from a radically different culture. The idea alone of using plants as a form of medicine is foreign, even those that have absolutely no psychoactive properties. Ayahuasca is known to help people dealing with a wide range of mental, emotional and physical health conditions including PTSD, depression, anxiety, stress and suicidal tendencies. These conditions are often resistant to treatment by conventional methods and require the patient to take pharmaceuticals or attend talk therapy sessions for the rest of their lives. Pharmaceuticals appear ineffective to say the least, and any illusion of their success comes from suppressing the symptoms rather than actually curing the root cause of the condition. Ayahuasca works in stark contrast, by helping the participant face the direct cause of their suffering, which allows them to process and eliminate it from their system. I should be careful when attempting to explain exactly how Ayahuasca brings healing because this advanced medicine works in mysterious ways that we may never fully understand. Besides, the focus of this book has never been to explain how Ayahuasca relieves suffering from a biochemical or psychological perspective. There are already plenty of books available written by MDs or PhDs that have more academic credentials than I do. The focus of this book has always been to document my personal experiences, a topic that nobody in the world has more qualifications for than me. More specifically, I examine the spiritual and mystical highs that arise during ceremony, a topic that science struggles to measure or quantify.

Having said all that, I do want to briefly talk about the healing qualities of this medicine. Suffering can be a gift. I know that statement doesn't seem to make sense at first glance, but we often avoid making major changes in our lives until there is absolutely no other option. Suffering forces us to try a different approach, sometimes in ways that are risky or scary. Sometimes in ways that are not accepted by our families, religions or societies. These are a few of the reasons why we avoid change, because it may require a new lifestyle that we or the people around us are initially not comfortable with. In my case the unexplainable skin reactions I was having to certain foods and the depression I felt at my job every day drove me to the Amazon in search of a cure. Quitting a stable job to go searching for shamanic rainforest medicine is not considered normal behavior in this society. It was scary because I had no idea where to go, what to do, or when my next paycheck would come, but I also knew it needed to happen. Not only did that courageous decision free me from depression, but it also led to a long list of blessings, including this book. Suffering can be a gift.

In Phoenyx's case PTSD drove her to seek Ayahuasca after many years of working as a police officer. Imagine that, police officers exist to enforce the law, and Ayahuasca is illegal in many countries around the world, yet her suffering drove her to drink anyway. It's actually not that difficult to imagine when you think of all the trauma and stress a job like that would produce. A year of Somatic Experience therapy had yielded no benefits. Thank God another therapist had the courage and compassion to recommend Ayahuasca after only a few sessions, advice that was very risky, and some might argue unprofessional. I would reply that a good therapist who truly understands psychology, the medicine and their patient, knows whether it is appropriate to make such a suggestion. The therapist even admitted that the alternative was probably thirty years of talk therapy, and that would only manage the symptoms, not cure the PTSD. After nine ceremonies in six months Phoenyx no longer had symptoms of PTSD. Five years later that is still the case. Eventually she too left her job and is now enjoying a lifestyle that is more in alignment with what truly inspires her. Suffering can be a gift.

As I mentioned earlier, the previous summer I had earned a certificate as a coach who specializes in helping people prepare for, navigate through and integrate after Sacred Medicine experiences. For clarification, I was not trained to provide illegal substances or sit with people under the influence of them. More specifically, the focus of the program was on using Sacred Medicines as a method for recovering from addiction. For example, the Ibogaine concentrate from the Iboga plant has proven successful for interrupting opiate cravings and withdrawal symptoms. It also allows the addict to face the cause of their addiction. What people sometimes fail to realize is that the addict is still responsible for integrating the experience. This means building a new lifestyle that supports independence from substances, which can be done with the assistance of a coach.

I really appreciate the organization's unique view of addiction. With conventional methods, true recovery typically never happens, instead abstinence is practiced with strict discipline until the person relapses and rotates in and out of hospitals, expensive treatment programs or the legal system. True recovery comes from making profound changes inside yourself. The idea is to go straight to the source and process the actual cause of the addiction, so that ultimately it's no longer necessary to rely solely on will power. As long as the source of the suffering remains, the potential for a relapse exists. So how does one heal the source of their suffering? As I mentioned in the first paragraph, Ayahuasca can help you do that, along with many other Sacred Medicines.

Let's take a closer look at this. During the training I was exposed to the phrase, "Catalyze your consciousness." A catalyst is a substance that increases the rate of a chemical reaction. For example, a plant such as Ayahuasca could help a person recover much faster than normal by catalyzing the expansion of their consciousness. As our awareness grows, so does our ability to clearly see what is holding us back. According to the training, the cause of suffering and the resulting addiction often comes from a disconnect. A person could be disconnected from nature, family, purpose or a healthy routine, but above all there is often a disconnect from the Higher Self. As I've been saying throughout much of this book, Ayahuasca allows me to connect with the Higher Self that emerges when the rational mind is reduced. When a person achieves true recovery by healing the source of their suffering, and connecting to their Higher Self, they can receive much more than the mere absence of an addiction. Initially they might wish to simply return to their old life prior to addiction, but eventually they may create a new life that is much greater than they could have ever imagined. In fact, one will probably find it undesirable or even impossible to return to their old lifestyle. Suffering is a gift because it provides fuel for growth.

In the first chapter I introduced the theme of the book based on lyrics written by Trey Anastasio, "There must be something more than this," so what exactly is he referring to? I can't speak for Trey, but I have an interpretation of what *this* is. There must be something more than this depression, PTSD and addiction. There must be something more than these sedentary, repetitive, unsatisfying jobs. There must be something more than this consuming, wasting, polluting society. There must be something more than climate change, habitat destruction and species extinction. There must be something more than artificially-flavored, pesticide-sprayed, factory-raised food. There must be something more than ___fill in the blank___. And there is, if we can somehow Wake Up! Unfortunately, the growth of the society may need to follow the same course as the growth of the individual. In other words, just as the addict needs to suffer through the loss of their job, friends and health before they decide to seek change, perhaps humanity needs to experience war, overpopulation and economic collapse? I sure hope not, but unless Sacred Medicines are removed from the schedule of controlled substances and made more easily available then I'm afraid mainstream society will only seek them after disaster strikes. Wouldn't it be better to prevent disease than react to it?

If suffering is a gift that fuels our growth then what happens when there is no suffering at the individual level (or at least awareness or acceptance of it)? Many Americans are enjoying the comforts bought by their wealth, and let's face it, nobody wants to change when they are comfortable. When people are protected by their wealth, obsessed with their possessions and distracted by their technology, they tend to be insulated from the world around them. I suppose one of the biggest challenges we face is convincing people that personal change is necessary. We're all aware of the problems facing humanity, but we often see them as caused by others. We also seem to expect scientists and politicians to solve all our problems, but we can never design or vote our way out of this situation. The reality is that we all contribute to the problem, just as we can all contribute to the solution. And how do I propose we do that? You guessed it, by expanding our consciousness, healing our traumas and changing our lives through the responsible use of Sacred Medicines. Despite temporary illusions of happiness produced by consumerism, I suspect that hidden underneath artificial, pharmaceutical smiles there remains an emptiness that we try to fill with material possessions. A dissatisfaction, or as I mentioned earlier, a disconnect from the Higher Self. The rich may not struggle with scarcity, but they still need to face their inner demons at the end of the day. Why do you think we often see famous, successful people committing suicide or addicted to drugs? Because money buys comfort, but it doesn't buy deep fulfillment. Suffering is fuel for growth.

When I was younger I went through a phase of fighting against the system by expressing my anger and focusing on all the mistakes we are collectively making. I was trying to "save the world." Now I don't feel obligated to convince anybody that the train is heading full speed towards the cliff. Following my first trip to Peru there has been a shift from improving the world to improving myself. Always raging against the machine is a waste of energy that could be better spent elsewhere. For example, now I find a much better approach is to present an alternative path for people to walk down, at least that is the intention of writing this book. Rather than tell people what not to do, how about showing them a better option that they can do? In fact, I don't think it's even necessary to push them in one direction or another. If you give someone the choice of either continuing to drink dirty water from a stagnant pond, or trying a crystal-clear, glacier-fed stream instead, then there is no convincing necessary. The choices speak for themselves. I believe that Sacred Medicines could greatly improve the chance of our species surviving this dangerous moment in history. They have the potential to give our speeding train wings for flight. They are the glass of pure water. They are catalysts.

At the university I studied Environmental Science and as a result tend to view the overall health of the human species based on the state of the natural environment. After all, the Earth is our home, and what sane person would destroy their own home? Looking at the situation through my green-tinted glasses I often wondered what strategy would work best to protect our last remaining wild areas. Should we rely on governments, non-profit organizations or corporations? Then one day I thought about where I would donate my money if I ever became super wealthy. Would it be the Nature Conservancy, Sierra Club or the Rainforest Action Network? No. I'm sure they all do great work, but for me the best way of protecting the environment would be to donate my money to a psychedelic advocacy organization such as the Multidisciplinary Association for Psychedelic Studies (MAPS). It may sound strange, but things like laws, economic incentives and protests will only get us half way there. To truly change the world we need to change our minds, and the fastest way of doing that is with a catalyst like Ayahuasca. In my opinion, there is literally no other method on planet Earth that accelerates transformation more than consuming Sacred Medicines.

Despite all this talk of the potential for Sacred Medicines to protect our environment, improve our health and save the world from destruction, I never promised it would be easy. Working with Ayahuasca means much more than to simply swallow the medicine. If people are looking for an easy pill then the pharmaceutical industry has plenty of options available. I guess after decades of conditioning we have come to expect solutions that are convenient and don't require any changes in our busy lives, but that's not how Ayahuasca works. The healing process can be messy and uncomfortable. The ultimate question any person considering this path must answer is whether you want large amounts of short term suffering, or small amounts of long term suffering. The former will likely be painful yet effective, while the latter typically manages the symptoms, but never results in a solution. Ask Phoenyx how comfortable she was facing her PTSD during those nine ceremonies in six months that forever transformed her life for the better. It was at times torturous, yet totally worth it. Ultimately people need to want to change, because without that desire no pill or plant will ever be enough. Having legal access to medicine at least empowers people to make the decision of whether or not to proceed.

The good news is that awareness of Sacred Medicines is improving as they appear in more books, movies and podcasts. Research is expanding at major universities, and organizations like MAPS have an excellent chance of receiving Food and Drug Administration approval to use psychedelic substances for therapy. Social media is spreading the word all around the world one post at a time. Religions and indigenous groups are fighting for continued access to their sacraments. The state-by-state legalization of Cannabis in the US is opening minds to the use of plants as medicines. Celebrities are coming out of the Psychedelic Closet. Despite all of these positive developments the question remains of whether we will prevent a global catastrophe, or react to it. I think the answer depends on how quickly we end decades of prohibition against Sacred Medicines.

☿

Beyond Healing

If you reached this last chapter of the book it should be clear by now that healing was not the primary reason for drinking Ayahuasca in Brazil. Phoenyx's symptoms of PTSD had disappeared long before we ever agreed to be caretakers, and while my food allergies were not yet cured I had learned to live with them. Some readers must be wondering why we continued to drink at the rate we did after our original goals were satisfied. After all, one of the major differences between pharmaceuticals and Ayahuasca is that the former need to be taken continuously to suppress the symptoms while the latter is not needed anymore after the source of the suffering has been processed. If you can recall, there was another reason I took that first trip to the Amazon a few years prior, to treat depression related to an unsatisfying job. Ayahuasca certainly helped interrupt the depression, but as I like to say, swallowing is the easy part. The most important step in the healing process is to return home and integrate the insights you gained during ceremony by making actual changes in your daily routine. In my case I was open and more than ready to try something different, but I wasn't looking for any ordinary job since that was the original cause of the depression. I realized that returning to the old paradigm would never bring me satisfaction. Ever since I graduated from high school I have been on a lifelong mission to find a career that not only paid the bills, but also one that supported my health, matched my interests and felt rewarding. As if that wasn't idealistic enough, I wanted to earn an income by contributing to a better world, instead of exploiting people or planet. Good luck finding that, eh? Working in the environmental field looked like the right place for me, but it turns out there is much more money to be made destroying wilderness than protecting it. Besides, working for others didn't match my personality very well. It took many years to finally understand that I was searching for my purpose, not a career.

A couple years before that first trip to Peru, I was introduced to a man who provided Jyotish readings. Jyotish is a system of astrology from India that can be used to align your life with the current position of the planets relative to their location at your time of birth. I paid for a session that provided guidance on Dharma, which means life purpose. The Jyotishi explained to me that most people choose their profession based on rational factors such as salary or societal expectations, and that this is one of the greatest mistakes we can make. He also said that writing would be a good match for me, and if I wrote a book then it would definitely sell. I resonated with the idea and decided to start a blog. The book would have to wait five more years until the right topic came to my attention. To make a long story short, Ayahuasca did interrupt my depression, but I continued drinking it in order to find my professional role in the Sacred Medicine scene. Ultimately this pursuit led to Norberto's invitation to be caretakers in Brazil, which provided an abundance of material to write my first book. The completion of this book feels more like a beginning than an ending. Who knows what else it will lead to? As I align with my Dharma and accomplish my lifelong mission to earn an income in a sustainable way by helping others improve their lives, memories of depression fade away.

The original theme of the book was, "There must be something more than this," and as I transition to my new role of author those words sound truer than ever. While the quote started for me as a reference to a mundane job or lifestyle, it quickly evolved to take on other meanings. I introduced a modified theme in the "Active Participation" chapter, "There must be something more than this" overactive, rational mind. And there is, for me it appears approximately three to four hours after I drink Ayahuasca. This is the time when the rational mind has already powered down and the Higher Self emerges. As I've said throughout the book, my basic assumption is that consciousness is broken into two components, the rational mind and the Higher Self. Perhaps that is an overly simplistic explanation, but at least it gives us a language to work with. I have often sung praise for the Higher Self, though words are insufficient until you experience it directly. Regardless, I can do my best to describe why somebody would want to live in it more often: It feels like stepping off a crowded street and entering a silent room. It feels like your mind has just been given a hot oil massage and is now releasing the tension of its muscles after a long day of difficult work. It feels like waking up from ten hours of deep sleep without the fogginess. It feels like different parts of my brain are communicating that usually do not. Creative thoughts appear effortlessly and seem to have a quality of deep truth that inspires confidence and trust to take appropriate action. Paradoxically, I feel more sober in that altered state than I do when I'm... sober. It's realer than what we usually consider reality. It feels like the baseline, a place we should always return to whenever we stray. Peace. Not that cliché version you have heard a thousand times, but actual peace. It feels like this is who I am. These are some of my inadequate attempts to explain why we continue to drink, and go Beyond Healing.

You might be wondering whether my mantra from the "Active Participation" chapter worked:

"The rational mind is no longer dominant over the Higher Self.

The Higher Self is now in control.

The rational mind will take the role of servant to the Higher Self."

Or my technological mantra from the "Eat Me, Delete Me" chapter:

"Delete any unnecessary programs and files from my human operating system that prevent me from regularly accessing higher states of consciousness during my daily life."

I'd love to report that I now stand in line at the grocery store feeling as elevated and connected as I do lying on my mattress in the temple, unfortunately that is not the case. Does that mean Active Participation, the ability to reprogram ourselves with the assistance of Ayahuasca, has failed? Absolutely not. The benefits are definitely arriving, and after only a few months back in the US the integration process is still incomplete. What I find most noticeable is the ability to be present in daily situations, or at least to recognize when the presence is interrupted by a recurring pattern. For example, I may behave impatiently and then become aware of it shortly after, or even better while it is happening. I'm not sure if it's possible to vibrate with energy throughout my daily routine the way I sometimes do during a profound ceremony, but I'm certain that enhanced awareness has already happened, and that alone is major progress compared to how most people are living these days. One major insight I've had about the process is that perhaps the mantras don't automatically do exactly what you ask them to do, instead they imprint you in that highly impressionable state with the conviction to follow through on your intention. In other words, asking for awakening may not instantly give you awakening, but it could reprogram you to continually give your best effort to awaken in any situation life presents you with. So Ayahuasca is not a genie in the bottle who grants anything you wish for, but she does meet you half way if you're willing to do some work.

Even though it should be obvious, I probably need to elaborate on how people must complete a majority of their healing process before they go beyond it. Many if not most people who have consumed psychedelics during the past fifty years have very likely skipped the healing part. After psychedelics were banned by the US government and medical research was abandoned, they primarily became a tool for getting high at concerts and parties. Look at the connection between MDMA and electronic dance music for a great example. Not that I have a problem with combining psychedelics and beautiful music, but the healing potential was often lost behind the flashing lights and booming speakers. When the healing process is skipped, a concept known as Spiritual Bypassing can occur. This becomes evident in people who have their head in the clouds, but no feet on the ground. Accessing psychic powers may sound like fun, but it can be very unbalanced when you haven't learned to deal with basic issues here on planet Earth, like being honest to others. No matter how high we ascend, we will always be pulled back down to the areas that still need work.

Currently organizations like MAPS are spending a majority of their resources on research that demonstrates how psychedelic therapy can heal sick people. For obvious strategic reasons MAPS decided to start with the people most desperately in need of help. A request sent to the Food and Drug Administration to legalize psychedelics so relatively healthy people can expand their consciousness, transcend to alternate dimensions and communicate with spirits, probably would have been laughed at and ignored. However, an attempt to heal Iraq war veterans suffering from PTSD demands attention. Ultimately I think we can all benefit from these substances, whether or not we receive a diagnosis for a condition. They provide unlimited opportunities to learn, grow and evolve on a spiritual level. I hope that eventually it will be more common for so-called healthy people to have access to Sacred Medicines, with or without a therapist.

Until that day comes people will either need to visit countries where Sacred Medicines are legal, seek protection under the freedom of religion or commit a crime. I suppose you could also wait until the laws change, but I don't think we can afford to live like this any longer. In the case of Steve Jobs I'm glad that he decided to commit a crime. Steve reminds us of the tremendous possibilities that arise from the consumption of psychedelics. He claims that, "Taking LSD was a profound experience, one of the most important things in my life." The implications of that statement are enormous when you consider that the products he created have changed our lives in radical ways. It makes me wonder what other amazing breakthroughs are waiting to grow in bright fertile minds once the seeds of expansion have been planted. Unfortunately when Steve went beyond, he appeared to have mostly skipped the healing. Based on accounts I read about his personality and untimely death, I believe psychedelic therapy could have helped him immensely. He once tried primal scream therapy, though as we have all heard about his legendary temper, it didn't seem to help much. Imagine if he had the opportunity to participate in a male lineage release exercise with Norberto, and was able to purge an *Incredible Hulk* yell as I did. You can't really blame the guy as psychedelic therapy evaporated once we entered the dark ages of prohibition. Sacred Medicines are catalysts that not only accelerate the healing process, but also apparently increase innovation, creativity and the rate of technological development, which is why software engineers microdose LSD in Silicon Valley. What other inventions would we have if Steve were still alive today?

Speaking of microdosing, in a book focused on the Modern Mind I think it's worth briefly mentioning the Optimization community that seems to be getting more popular lately. There are loads of performance-enhancing supplements available at the grocery store or online. Some of these are called Nootropics or smart drugs, and others are herbal formulas. Many podcasts and websites now offer an abundance of information on biohacking techniques that are meant to maximize efficiency, increase energy or sharpen mental clarity. Humans always strive to go further, either as ultra endurance athletes, Wall Street bankers or those interested in general self-improvement. Personally, I am fascinated with the concept of Optimization, but I believe the danger we face here is in further strengthening an already powerful rational mind prior to recognizing the proper role of the Higher Self. Look to the movie *Limitless* for an example of a man who uses a pill to enhance his mind and transform from below average to a wealthy politician, rather than choosing to awaken. In our capitalistic society it is inevitable that Nootropics will primarily be used to gain a competitive advantage and earn more money. Sacred Medicines can allow us to go Beyond Healing into the realm of Optimization, which could also lead to the pursuit of greater profit. However, I think the difference between the two methods is that Sacred Medicines can fundamentally shift the way we perceive the world. Hopefully a person who develops the capacity to defeat their so-called opponents, can simultaneously appreciate that there are more important things in life than collecting money, and then direct their attention towards a new priority. Or they may have a sudden realization that their methods for making money were harming people and planet, and then attempt to switch to a more sustainable business model. Unfortunately this is not always the case. There are no guarantees that Sacred Medicines will inspire all who partake to transition from the old to new paradigm. If a person simply uses them as a tool to continue business as usual then I believe they have completely missed the target.

We've reached a point now where the dominance of the modern mind on our lifestyle has exceeded the limits of what our planet can tolerate. Inevitably an invention that dwarfs Jobs' LSD-inspired iPhone is looming somewhere over the horizon, but in my opinion the never-ending development of the rational mind does not create a future we can thrive in. Tesla founder Elon Musk gave us the electric car to help ease our transition to a better future. While he already does the work of ten men, we would probably need a thousand Elon Musks to set us on a sustainable course. In other words, I simply don't believe that we can invent our way out of this mess. It's time for the great human mind to bow down to a wiser form of consciousness, the Higher Self. I'm not suggesting we return to living in caves and reading by candlelight, but that we use our rational mind as a powerful tool. Let the wisdom of the Higher Self determine how and when it is appropriate to use that tool. For example, we are capable of extracting coal from the Earth to generate energy and make profit, that's an easy challenge for our best engineers to solve. But should we, or can we collectively agree that living in harmony with our planet is a better option? It is quite common for people to gain appreciation and respect that they never previously had for Pachamama, or Mother Nature, during an Ayahuasca experience. Sacred Medicines can help us move

Beyond Healing of our illnesses and towards a more technologically advanced and environmentally friendly existence.

I suppose there are people who agree with my message of Beyond Healing, but disagree with my methods. Better health for the individual, better health for the society, protecting the environment, finding our purpose in life, experiencing mystical highs, growing, learning, evolving, yes, yes, yes, all good. Yet many who call themselves spiritual would not understand the need to consume Sacred Medicines for assistance. We can do it without the use of chemicals they say, through methods such as yoga, breath work, chanting, meditation, fasting, etc. I agree, there are many different paths to awakening, and that's great if you find one that works for you. Let's just be clear though about where the opposition to assistance comes from. Could it perhaps come from fifty years of prohibition and social conditioning? Further examination would probably reveal conditioning that goes back centuries rather than decades with the church's systematic destruction of indigenous, shamanic and earth centered traditions. What once was considered a holy sacrament has been turned into a forbidden fruit.

When asked about achieving mystical highs without plants, psychedelic philosopher Terence McKenna replied, "My God, who would want to? What would be proved by achieving these things without drugs? …Humble yourself to the point of making a deal with a plant." The refusal to accept help from nature sounds very confused and arrogant to me. Why not extend this resistance to our need for food?

"Sorry, I don't eat vegetables, I can survive independently." Do people think they are somehow above the plant kingdom? We come from nature, we are nature. If fruits exists to provide us with physical nourishment then perhaps the purpose of Sacred Medicines is to provide us with spiritual nourishment, or as Terence calls it, Food of the Gods. Let's turn this around now. The question should not be, why do you consume psychedelics, I think it's more important to ask, why are you *not* consuming them?! A majority of our problems wouldn't exist if humans regularly ate Sacred Medicines as they have for thousands of years. That may sound like a bold statement, but it seems very obvious to me. We've removed a giant societal mirror that previously helped us examine whether our lives were in alignment with our moral compass, and in balance with our environment.

An argument coming from spiritual circles seems to be that many of the great masters came from India, the land that gave us many tools for awakening, and they didn't ever depend on chemicals to expand consciousness. Actually that statement sounds ridiculous when you consider that India also gives us Ayurveda, an ancient system of medicine that includes a masterful knowledge of plants. I can't take seriously the idea that these people who dedicated their entire lives to awakening, and were also experts in the field of plant medicine, would pass the opportunity to consume a plant in order to fulfill their mission. The Rig Veda is a holy book that almost obsessively sings the praise of a mysterious plant formula known as Soma that produces mystical states. Why meditate in a cave for fifty years to reach enlightenment when you can have the same results in a single day with Sacred Medicines? As I've already mentioned, these substances are catalysts that accelerate the awakening process. Most importantly, we don't have the luxury of waiting fifty years for society to awaken from cave meditation.

I'm not suggesting Tibetan Buddhist monks were eating psilocybin mushrooms every day, but to have such an experience certainly gives a person a preview of where they are headed. According to sixties counter cultural leader Ram Dass, his guru Neem Karoli Baba shared the following, "With psychedelics you could go into the room in which Christ and Buddha exist, but you only stay for a few minutes." An important reminder that consuming these substances alone will not bring us enlightenment. At first glance Neem Karoli Baba seems to be describing a limitation of psychedelics, yet what a gift those few minutes must be for a person who may not have otherwise had that experience in their entire life. I think this is one of the greatest strengths of Sacred Medicines. Not everybody is willing to drink Ayahuasca as often as Phoenyx and I did last winter, but to have at least one profound experience can provide inspiration to walk a spiritual path. Better yet, why not combine the two? Sacred Medicines with spiritual teachings and practices from Asia, or other parts of the world, complement each other and don't need to be used exclusively.

I guess that when philosopher Alan Watts said, "When you get the message, hang up the phone," he too was warning of the limitations of psychedelics. I respect the man, but people sometimes use this famous quote to imply that psychedelics should only be used as an introduction to spirituality. My first reaction is, "Let's keep talking!" Perhaps Alan should have added, "…And then pick it back up again when you're ready for more." Should I honestly believe I can receive all the teachings of the universe in a single phone call?

Let's not forget that our society is highly dependent on drugs, mostly those that have been deemed appropriate by authorities. Is it a coincidence that the drugs classified as legal are those that make us more productive workers, like caffeine and nicotine, or those that sedate us from the pains of daily living like alcohol and opiates? Of course there's nothing wrong with working hard, especially when you enjoy what you do. But if you are struggling to survive, hate your job and depend on medication to get through the week then there might be a problem. We work to live and live to work. Meanwhile the psychedelic drugs that demand deep introspection and critical thinking are prohibited. In the land of the free and home of the brave, slavery still exists. While nobody wears shackles around their ankles, a majority of us wear them firmly locked around our minds. In case this is all sounding a little bit dramatic, imagine putting a person in prison for eating a plant, that to me is more dramatic by many orders of magnitude. Phoenyx and I have chosen to consume Sacred Medicines after we were cured because it is our birthright. The freedom to do what you wish with your consciousness is a gift that was taken long ago. It is your duty to take it back.

Last but not least, to continue drinking medicine and go Beyond Healing is a reminder of the truly important things in life. In this culture it's so easy to get sucked back into the illusion that dominates our culture. The narrative of society that says, we've got it all figured out, the secret to life is to work hard, listen to authority and consume material possessions. Even after a powerful weekend workshop the return home can quickly cause us to struggle when the insights gained conflict with our daily routine. To drink Sacred Medicines regularly and go Beyond Healing can be a good strategy for balancing the forces of our society that tend to pull us back down from the Higher Self to the rational mind. Now that national holidays have become nothing more than heavily commercialized excuses for a day off work, rituals are missing in our culture. We still have birthdays, anniversaries, graduations and weddings, but I think we are missing a regular practice of reconnection. This is what most churches attempt, but fail to offer (excluding Santo Daime of course). Events like full moon celebrations and solstice ceremonies provide an opportunity to transcend this physical existence and experience the great mystery.

Back in the first chapter I declared that this book is not about me. While it appears at first glance to only be a personal account of my psychedelic journey in Brazil, it's also a book for anybody who considers walking this path. The primary reason I wrote this is actually to awaken the reader to the possibility that you too can do the same. I obviously can't provide step-by-step instructions because that would lead you to my purpose, not yours. However, I can share these words whole heartedly: be courageous dear reader, follow your passion, and be willing to swim upstream like a salmon against the current of mainstream society.

"Climb up

Over the top

Survey the state of the soul

You've got to find out

For yourself

Whether or not you're truly trying

Why not

Give it a shot

Shake it, take control

And inevitably wind up

And find out for yourself

All the strengths

That you have inside of you"

-Song for a Friend, by Jason Mraz

☿

Further

Operating Systems

For the record, and for whatever it's worth to the reader, Phoenyx has insisted since the moment she first saw me that I was different, or as we like to joke that I have a different operating system than most other people. Her keen sense of personality analysis that she developed after years of working as a police officer instantly detected my unusual ways of being within hours of meeting. She believes I am operating at the high-functioning end of the autism spectrum, also known as Asperger's syndrome. So am I? Perhaps I am simply an introvert, or maybe my communication skills are the result of growing up as an only child. When Phoenyx first met me my behavior could have been influenced by my job-related depression, or the trauma resulting from serving in the military. An online test developed by the Cambridge Autism Research Centre indicated there is a high probability that I am on the spectrum. We considered getting a professional diagnosis, but decided not to due to the outrageously high cost of health care in the US and my lack of insurance for the past three years. It may have been a waste of money anyway because as I am about to explain, my unique situation could easily produce a false negative diagnosis from the doctor.

According to one psychologist I spoke with, Asperger's is more easily identified during the younger developmental years of life because over time adults learn strategies for adapting to the world neurotypicals have created, which makes it more difficult to identify an atypical person. Perhaps the most effective strategy I learned for adapting to this world is to regularly drink powerful Sacred Medicines. Phoenyx says she has observed a radical transformation since we first met. I would never make such a bold statement that I found the cure for Asperger's. Actually, I don't think this condition needs to be cured at all, but perhaps Sacred Medicines can smooth the rough edges that make communication between neurotypicals and atypicals difficult? These substances seem to enhance our ability to relate to others on an emotional level, a capability that is notoriously underdeveloped in people with Asperger's. Sacred Medicines certainly help us to look within and recognize how we are interacting with our surroundings, and there is no doubt in my high-functioning mind that they exist to improve our lives. My theory is that Sacred Medicines help to silence the rational mind, regardless of which operating system the person has, and the resulting Higher Self that then emerges can communicate more effectively. In that case our Higher Selves act as master translators, or better yet, they speak a universal language.

To be honest, I was hesitant to include this section because of the uncertainty from not having a proper diagnosis, and the possibility that some might mistakenly believe I have a disability. It's certainly not a disability, in fact I would argue that neurodiversity benefits the human species by contributing new perspectives to our culture. I also saved this information for last because I didn't want it to influence the reader's view of our initiation. While I never intended to have my operating system as the main focus of the book, I do think it's worth at least mentioning, especially for the readers and their family members who are also dealing with it. I sometimes hear questions about whether Sacred Medicines are appropriate for people with Asperger's. The organization MAPS has been researching the use of MDMA-assisted therapy for social anxiety in autistic adults. However, MDMA is relatively gentle in comparison with an Ayahuasca experience. Since sensitivity to inputs can be a symptom of autism, some may wonder whether the visuals would be too much for a person to handle. Personally, I am very sound sensitive, but at no point have I ever thought Ayahuasca was incompatible with my nervous system. In fact, I find a visit to a crowded city street to be much more stressful. My recommendation for a person on the spectrum wanting to explore Sacred Medicines, but not sure if it's a good idea, would be the same as what I would tell anybody who is hesitant; simply start small and slowly increase in dose. Just remember that if at some point it becomes challenging, this is very common during an Ayahuasca ceremony, regardless of what type of operating system you have.

We may never know whether or not I am on the edge of the spectrum, especially as I continue to upgrade with each passing ceremony. I now feel more comfortable in conceding that I may sit at the high-functioning end, especially with my discovery of admirable people who admit to, or are suspected of perceiving the world in a different way. One thing I do know is that we have barely scratched the surface of exploring the great potential these substances have to offer in treating a wide variety of conditions. Ultimately, we all exist along one type of spectrum or another, and the best way of dealing with it is to look within and know ourselves better, a practice that is greatly enhanced through the responsible and safe use of Sacred Medicines.

Cover Art

Explaining the meaning of art is often a questionable act since it's usually better to let the art speak for itself. However, I just want to say a few words about the wonderful cover that Eugenia Werner has created. This collaboration is the result of my request to see a visual representation of:

"India meeting Brazil,
the Ganges meeting the Amazon,
the Himalayas meeting the Andes,
meditation meeting medication,
and religion meeting spirituality"

The Buddha statue comes from a sacred site in Sedona, Arizona, a place Phoenyx and I wintered a couple years ago while I was volunteering as an Ayurvedic cook for budding yoga instructors in training. The Amitabha Stupa where the Buddha resides was only a few blocks from our studio, so we would walk there frequently. It is said that one should walk in clockwise circles around the Stupa in multiples of three, a practice we did countless times while expressing gratitude for all the blessings we had received, and requesting guidance for future endeavors.

While this Buddha was chosen specifically for the direct role it played in my life, it wasn't until the final minutes before publishing that a friend explained to me the significance of this statue. He told me that there are actually different types of Buddhas and each is distinguished by its pose and hand gestures. Apparently the Amitabha Stupa is home to a "Teaching Buddha," which is depicted by the index finger and thumb touching on both hands. Even more interesting was the discovery that there is also another statue called "Medicine Buddha" who holds a bowl (or glass) in his left hand. When I had asked Eugenia to place one of our ceremonial glasses in his left hand during the design process, we unintentionally created a hybrid "Teaching-Medicine Buddha." This now seems very fitting as the book provides teachings about medicine. Another way of looking at this is that Ayahuasca is not only sought by many for medicinal purposes, but she also has the potential to be a teacher on many levels. I am surprised and delighted by the Buddhist interpretation of our creation, and once again am left wondering who or what really guided my decision.

Buddha's golden tint honors the Ourinho (little golden) Ayahuasca that we drank all winter in Brazil. There are Toé flowers below him, Chacruna leaves around him, and sliced Ayahuasca wood above and behind him. Although Toé grows on the property, and is a symbol of the rainforest, to be clear, it is NOT a plant that we or Norberto work with. At risk of stating the obvious, the glass in his hand represents the possibility that with the assistance of a plant, we too can have experiences as he once did, even if only for a day, a subject that is the central theme to the "Beyond Healing" chapter.

Gratitude

I offer my Gratitude to the following people:

- Jenny Coe for recognizing my talent and encouraging me to write.

- Dan Martin for joining me on my first trip to the Amazon, and the countless hours we have discussed many of the subjects presented in this book.

- Dennis Flaherty (Jyotishi) for explaining my Dharma (life purpose) as a writer.

- Todd Caldecott (Ayurvedic Practitioner) for successfully managing my diet as I searched for a permanent solution to food allergies.

- Josip Orlovac for introducing me to Huachuma.

- Norberto Jurasek for teaching me his style of facilitation, serving me high quality medicine and inviting me to care for his land.

- Grandfather Huachuma for all the healing and exploration.

- And of course Mother Ayahuasca for speaking through me.

To Phoenyx Petersen,

Thank you for sharing this amazing adventure. Every time I think we have reached the peak, we somehow find a way to go higher. Once again I ask, how can this be topped?

Gracias for understanding and appreciating me.

Obrigado for the many hours we spent editing together.

This book would not have been possible without your assistance. Rise from the ashes Phoenyx, the Sun phase of your life awaits you!

"Give forth thy light to all without doubt; the clouds and shadows are no matter for thee"

-*Aleister Crowley Thoth Tarot*, Sun card

Connections

If you hear the call then follow your bliss to Terramaya, the Ayahuasca healing center featured in this book and owned by our facilitator/shaman Norberto Jurasek. Visit his website and reserve your mattress for the next scheduled workshop.

https://www.terramaya.org

If you wish to work with me in any role including: ceremony facilitation, transformational coaching, tour guiding, speaking or interviews, then email me or visit my website. Coaching is highly recommended for preparing the participant before ceremony and supporting them in the integration after. Coaching allows us to maximize the benefits by turning the temporary states of ceremony into permanent traits of daily living.

sacredmedicineguide@protonmail.com

https://www.sacredmedicineguide.com

Note, there are also many beautiful photos from the book available at my website.

Phoenyx Petersen can be reached by email. phoenyx7@protonmail.com

The cover artist Eugenia Werner can be reached by email. eugenia.werner@protonmail.com

Playlist

Modern Music for the Sacred Medicine: the soundtrack to our movie. Songs played in and outside the temple during ceremony.

- Bassnectar - Seek & Destroy (remix)
- Desert Dwellers - The Great Mystery (album)
- Grateful Dead - Box of Rain, Ripple
- Jack Johnson - You and Your Heart
- Jason Mraz - Bella Luna, Have it All, Song for a Friend
- Jimi Hendrix Experience - Bold as Love
- Led Zeppelin - Immigrant Song
- Michael Giacchino - The Master of the Mystic (Doctor Strange soundtrack)
- OneRepublic - Love Runs Out, Ordinary Human
- Phish - Come Together / Rise Up, Mercury, More
- Pink Floyd - Interstellar Overdrive, Learning to Fly
- Porangui - Ayahuasca (album)
- TV on the Radio - Golden Age
- Visionary Shamanics - Bass Temple (album)

☿

Watchlist

Movies and shows that appeared in our movie:

- The Accountant
- Arrival
- Black Panther
- Breaking Bad
- Dexter
- Doctor Strange
- The Doors
- Fear and Loathing in Las Vegas
- The Fountain
- Inception
- Incredible Hulk
- Indiana Jones
- Innsæi
- Iron Man
- Limitless
- The Martian
- The Matrix
- Mr. Robot
- Thor

☿

Phoenyx smells her favorite flower

The author in the Andes Mountains of Peru

Made in the USA
Columbia, SC
24 July 2019